Alex Jordan

architect
of his own
dream

by Doug Moe

House of Wyoming Valley, Inc.
Spring Green, WI 53588

Alex Jordan - architect of his own dream
by Doug Moe

Published by the House of Wyoming Valley, Inc.
Spring Green, WI 53588

Cover Photograph: House On The Rock Archives

ISBN — 0-9630207-0-6

Contents

Forward

It is unfortunate, but all too often true, that a person never really receives the recognition and praise for his accomplishments until after that person is no longer with us. We seldom take the time to tell those we love and respect how much they are appreciated. We often don't realize how much we need someone until after they are taken from us.

Alex Jordan has brought joy and entertainment to millions of people with his unique attraction, the House On The Rock.

Over the years, he declined numerous interviews from a variety of media, for he chose to let his creation do the talking for him. Thus, it is his attraction that is raved about all over the world, but very few people really know much about the man who made it all possible — Alex Jordan.

Many of us were fortunate enough to have had the opportunity to work with Alex Jordan. He truly was a genius, but more importantly a friend. It is the sincere hope of all of us at the House On The Rock that this authorized biography will shed some true light on Alex's life, so you too can really understand the man behind it all.

When Alex first started building the House On The Rock, a lot of people thought he was crazy. However, he was courageous enough to take a chance and pursue his dream and we are all better for it.

The host of Ripley's Believe It Or Not closed their feature segment on the House On The Rock by saying, "Thank you Mr. Jordan, wherever you are."

Yes indeed, thank you Alex. We appreciate all you've done for us and miss you more than you'll ever know. This book is for you. Maybe now you'll get the praise you so rightfully deserve.

You left us with the perfect way to remember you — the House On The Rock. Rest assured, your dream lives on!

Julie M. Esser

House On The Rock
Acknowledgements

This book would not have been possible without the input from numerous people who really knew Alex the best, the people who worked with him to make the House On The Rock what it is today.

A great thanks goes out to Alex's lifelong companion Jennie Olson, for she was gracious enough to share some one-of-a-kind photographs of Alex as he was growing up.

In addition, G. Barry Telfair and his wife Frances, who reside in St. Louis, spent nearly 30 years photographing the House On The Rock as it evolved into Wisconsin's #1 tourist attraction. They too are to be commended for the great deal of time they spent documenting the growth of the House On The Rock through pictures. Their photos further enhance this publication, as do the photos of Rich Rygh of the Capital Times, Madison and Pat Ripp of Dimensions In Photography, Mineral Point.

A special thanks to Deb Pickett and her entire staff at Southwest Graphics, Darlington, for bringing this entire project together.

About the Author

Doug Moe has worked as a magazine journalist since graduating from the University of Wisconsin-Madison in 1979. Currently associate editor of <u>Madison Magazine</u>, the city magazine of Madison, Wisconsin, he has been a contributing editor to <u>Milwaukee Magazine</u> as well as a regular contributor to scores of other newspapers and periodicals.

Mr. Moe's magazine writing has earned him two Golden Gavel Awards for outstanding journalism from the State Bar of Wisconsin, and, in 1985, he was named "Best Local Writer" in a readers poll conducted by <u>Madison Magazine</u>.

Since 1986 Mr. Moe has done three commentaries a week on local issues for radio station WMAD-FM in Madison and now serves as permanent substitute host for "Madison's Morning News" on radio station WTDY-AM.

Mr. Moe is the author of the 1990 book, <u>Greater Madison: Meeting the 21st Century</u>. He resides with his wife, Bette, in Monona, Wisconsin.

Acknowledgements

Julie Esser and Sue Donaldson first approached me about writing this book, and were even good enough to listen to a suggestion or two I had about it.

Much of the book is the product of my own interviewing. For sharing their memories of Alex Jordan, sometimes at considerable length, I'd like to thank Greg Burke, Art Donaldson, Julie Esser, Homer Fieldhouse, Lynn Fieldhouse, Doug Finley, Neil Hanson, John Korb, Tom Kupsh, Don Martin, John Mitby, Mike Olp, Jennie Olson, and Paul Yank.

In addition, a tape of John Korb's and Neil Hanson's three-hour interview with the late Sid Boyum was made available.

Julie Esser did a heroic job of collecting the voluminous newspaper and magazine stories written about the House On The Rock over the years. I drew on many of them, with appropriate credit in the text.

On a few occasions I also drew on an unpublished essay on the House written by John Korb.

John Mitby allowed me to peruse the 20 years of House On The Rock business correspondence he has in storage at his law office, Greg Burke braved chilly temperatures to give me a guided tour of the House.

Finally, a team effort at the House helped nursemaid the manuscript through to the book you now hold in your hands.

Dedication

This book is for Jennie Olson
and for Bette and Emmy

1   **Larger Than Life**

People used to say that when he entered a room he almost set off sparks, such was the infusion of energy that accompanied him. He used that energy to create what over the years became Wisconsin's top tourist attraction, a place of mystery, excitement and head-stunning beauty. The House On The Rock is many things to many people, and so was its creator, Alex Jordan.

Even before his death in 1989, at 75, Jordan had become a true Wisconsin legend, one of the most fascinating and intriguing characters in the Midwest, a much-discussed figure who was both feared and respected.

Opinions on his magnum opus, the House On The Rock, are less varied. First opened to the public in 1960, today over a half million people annually tour the House, located seven miles south of Spring Green, Wisconsin.

They marvel at the remarkable union of nature and imagination. It says something that the House is most often described as "indescribable". It is an architectural wonder, but it's also doll houses, cannons, music machines, organs, animals and Oriental art. It's a living entity — a history lesson and a peek into the future. Small surprise that even before people finish their tour, they're curious about this Alex Jordan, the man who created it.

Not only were the tourists curious, the national media came calling often over the years, only to be turned away. Alex Jordan did not like or seek personal publicity, a fact that seems strange, if not bizarre, in our celebrity-obsessed country. As cartoonist Garry Trudeau observed, "The United States is the only place in the world where a failure to promote yourself is perceived as arrogance."

Talk show host Dick Cavett once wanted to interview Jordan, and contacted the longtime manager of the House, John Korb.

"How about it, Alex?" Korb asked. After all, how often do you get a shot at that kind of free national publicity?

Jordan looked as if a snake had tried to bite him. "Anonymity is my greatest commodity," he said. "It's the only thing I have and I'm going to fight like hell to keep it. Don't you, Korb, interrupt it."

Plenty of media came even without a chance to interview the maestro. The network prime-time television show "Ripley's Believe It Or Not" did a segment on the House. The hostess ended the show standing in front of one of the House's most popular exhibits, the World's Largest Carousel.

"Thank you, Alex Jordan," the hostess said, "wherever you are."

Where he was most often was someplace in the House watching his customers, noting their reactions. Occasionally — perhaps because his picture was in the House brochure — he'd be recognized. A tourist would approach the tall, massive man dressed in easy clothes and standing alone in a corner and say, "You're Alex Jordan!"

Without fail, the man would deny it. "I'm the plumber," he'd say. On another day he was the electrician.

John Korb remembers standing near Jordan one day when he was recognized. "No, that's my brother in the brochure. We look alike. I'm the plumber."

Jordan wasn't above saying something just to be mischievous. But he sincerely felt a need to be able to move facelessly among the people in the House. For it was his customers' reactions that, in a sense, Jordan lived for.

Greg Burke, currently general manager of the House On The Rock, says that while Jordan was an avid builder and collector, no exhibit truly came alive for

A well-dressed, much younger, Alex Jordan in a rare professional photograph. Photo provided by Jennie Olson.

House On The Rock sculptor, Tom Kupsh, proudly stands in front of yet another masterpiece — a 56 foot long cannon. Photo by G.B. Telfair.

him until he could see it bring delight to the eyes of the public.

"It wasn't whether he liked an exhibit or not," Burke says, "or whether we liked it. He had a ten minute test. If it was well-received in the first ten minutes after a project was done and a room was open, well, that was the response we lived with. He wanted to hear, 'Oh, wow! That's fantastic!' If he heard that, it was a success for life."

Naturally enough, Jordan's reluctance to avail himself of publicity only made him more intriguing. He became a larger than life figure, which in a way was

4

appropriate, for Jordan was a large man of vast appetites. A man who demanded a lot of himself and those around him — of life itself.

There's a country song by Billy Joe Shaver that includes the lyric, "Too much ain't enough." Too much was never enough for Alex Jordan.

One day in 1978, Tom Kupsh, the House On The Rock's gifted sculptor, was finishing a project — an eight-foot St. Bernard dog. Alex Jordan came by the workshop, which wasn't unusual. He stopped nearly every day to watch Kupsh work and discuss present and future projects.

On this day, since he was finishing the St. Bernard, Kupsh turned to Jordan and asked, "What do you want me to do next?"

Jordan pulled a crumpled drawing out of his pocket that looked as if he'd been carrying it for years.

"I want you to build the world's largest cannon," Jordan said.

Six months of intense labor later, Kupsh was putting the last touches on a remarkable 56-foot long cannon. Jordan was clearly pleased. He took Kupsh aside.

"You know," he said, "all my life it has been the same. If I was going to have a drink, it wasn't going to be just one. If I was down to three packs of cigarettes, I was panicked and had to go into town for seven or eight more. There's never been enough. My whole life I've never been able to get enough of anything."

He looked at the cannon and then back at the sculptor. "Finally," Jordan said, "enough. You did it. This cannon is enough."

It wasn't, of course. Before the month was out another half dozen ideas for projects would be percolating in his head. Maybe he'd just been on the late-night telephone to St. Louis and they had the most incredible collection of circus miniatures. Or he'd just received a catalog and he wouldn't believe the craftsmanship pictured in those dollhouses.

Don Martin who over a span of 32 years worked on virtually every House On The Rock exhibit, says, "He was a buildaholic. He wanted something bigger than everybody else. If he bought a collection of something, he wanted the biggest collection of it."

Sid Boyum, an on-and-off friend of Jordan's for nearly 60 years, said, "He developed a collector's complex.

He couldn't leave anything alone. He had to buy everything."

Kupsh, the sculptor, disagrees. He thinks it was the process of turning fantasy into reality that drove Jordan.

"It wasn't only a question of how many and how big," Kupsh says. "It was a question of how wild could you be in your head and then actually get it out there."

Perhaps feeding his creativity, Jordan was a voracious reader. At one time Jordan subscribed to 38 periodicals, including National Geographic, Playboy, the Wall Street Journal, and of all things, the National Lampoon and Mad magazine.

Jordan's lifelong companion, Jennie Olson, says that one of his favorite publications was the Pumper, a journal devoted to the sewage disposal industry.

"He was a book man," Don Martin says of Jordan. "Every project we had, he'd immerse himself in it. Music machines? I think he got every book in the United States on music machines. In the world, probably. Then one year he got interested in steam engines, and it was the same thing again. That's just the way he was. He had his nose in a book all the time."

John Korb says of Jordan, "He was the most aware person in a wide variety of fields you'd ever find."

Arthur Donaldson, a Janesville businessman, who in 1988 purchased the House On The Rock, says simply, "I've met a lot of people in my life, and he was the most interesting man I ever met."

As is the case with any powerful personality, Jordan had his share of enemies, some of them well-earned. Alex Jordan was never an angel. He had a mercurial temper. He could be brusk, and on his bad days, cruel toward associates. There were times he cut corners and ignored good advice. He was, among all his other qualities, a stubborn man.

John Korb, manager of the House On The Rock for much of the 1970s and '80s, knew Jordan for 42 years. Talking with Korb, it's clear Jordan had a profound impact on his life.

"Of all the people I've met," Korb says, and he's met his share, having traveled to 65 countries, "Alex was undoubtedly the most complex man I've ever known. He created more of an ambivalent feeling in me than anyone I ever knew. He could arrive on the job in such a mood, so pleasant, that you just wanted to embrace him. You know, you were grateful for the inspiration you got from working with him. Twenty minutes later you wanted to deck him. He'd be a jerk — condescending. Then before he'd leave he'd do something redeeming."

One of the most-repeated stories about Jordan involves his parsimony when it came to paying employees. With a few exceptions, he did not like giving raises.

"He was just that way," Don Martin says. "He figured if someone didn't want to work here, he'd find someone else who did."

But it's vital to an understanding of Jordan to realize he was not going on tropical cruises or buying fancy clothes with the profits from the House. He was continually putting the money back into it — expanding, upgrading, creating.

"For a rich man he lived about as simple a life as anyone could live," Martin says. "He never took a vacation as long as I knew him. The House was his love and joy. He was one in a million. He gave his heart and soul to this place."

Jordan could, without question, be a tough man to work for. Greg Burke explains, "He probably was lacking in what you think of as people skills. You've got to realize all of Alex's energies were geared toward creativity."

It could produce some scenes which in hindsight become comical. One winter day Jordan pulled into the House parking lot and spotted a workman spreading salt on some icy patches. Well, that salt cost money that could be going toward a new exhibit!

Tom Kupsh recalls: "He immediately told the guy to stop. He darn near fired the guy. But that day as he was leaving, Alex slipped and fell on the ice. The next day he arrived with his van full of salt."

Kupsh says it wasn't unusual for Jordan to burst into a workshop and have two guys fired before he made it to the back door, never breaking stride.

"There were a lot of people who got fired who didn't really get fired," Korb says. He remembers one workman who Jordan bounced on a Tuesday. That Thursday, Jordan approached Korb.

"Where's so and so?" Jordan asked. "I haven't seen him around."

"Well," Korb said, "you fired him on Tuesday."

"What the hell did I do that for?" Jordan roared. "Get him back."

He could, on the other hand, be very generous with those people he liked and trusted. Art Donaldson, who knew Jordan for 15 years before buying the House in 1988, observes, "He could be very precise in what he wanted, but he could turn around and surprise you with his generosity."

Donaldson thinks Jordan may have been a little shy about this generosity. "He'd say, 'I don't want people to think I'm foolish.' I'd tell him, 'Alex, if you want to be nice that's not being foolish.' "

And Sid Boyum recalled, "He did a lot of good things that he didn't want credit for."

Boyum himself died this past February. In an interview for this book, he remembered something Jordan did for the high school and college kids who were helping him summers during the early years constructing the House.

"I used to see him give those kids money to go to school with at the end of the season," Boyum said. "He'd go over to the kids who had helped and give them $100 or $200 in cash, and say, 'This is for your education.' "

Boyum added, "If you were sick on the job, Alex would pick you up, put you in the car and drive you to the doctor or hospital."

Jordan would surprise employees with unexpected bonuses, often before Christmas. Jordan and his sculptor, Tom Kupsh, had a close relationship. When he heard Kupsh's daughter was beginning piano lessons, he gave him a piano. When Jordan's friend and attorney, John Mitby, of Madison, closed the sale of the House, Jordan gave him a valuable dollhouse for his kids.

It was Mitby who handled Jordan's estate, in which he left over $1 million to his most valued employees, and, as Mitby says, "paid the taxes on it."

That was appropriate, for those employees who endured, who helped Jordan realize and perpetuate his dream, meant as much to him as family, if not more.

Don Martin, who spent most of his adult life working with Jordan, is not a man given to sentimentality. Still, he says, "It's remarkable when you think about it. A little place like this, hidden in the woods, to have become so popular . . . ."

How much did the House mean to Jordan? His attorney, John Mitby, recalls, "After it was sold, and he received whatever funds it was that he was to receive, he took some of his own money to fix certain things, to dress them up the way he wanted them done. He just put it back into the House." He may have sold it, but it was still his.

Alex Jordan attacked life with an earthy swagger. In doing so, he became a legendary figure, but he was, in the end, a most human being, full of contradictions — kind, cruel, bold, shy, a showman and a private man.

Sid Boyum said, "He was a character. I liked his workmanship. He had a streak in him I don't believe anyone will ever have again. He had an innovative mind, and he knew how to use it. People like that are few and far between today."

At the time of his death, Jordan was still making plans for future innovations at the House On The Rock.

John Mitby says, "He felt an obligation to the people who bought a ticket to give them an experience they could not acquire anywhere else in the world."

Alex Jordan spent a lifetime trying to fulfill that obligation.

Alex Jordan's father, Alexander P. Jordan, and mother, Mary Magdelina Jordan. Photo provided by Jennie Olson.

2   The Early Years

His mother's name was Mary Magdelina Pregler and his father was Alexander P. Jordan. They were married in 1911 at the St. James Roman Catholic Church, Madison.

Alex Sr.'s family were farmers near Roxbury, a small town northwest of Madison, and were of modest means. He came to Madison as a young man to join his brothers in the meat business.

On his mother's side, the Pregler family "owned half of the Greenbush (an Italian neighborhood just off Madison's isthmus)," in the words of one woman who knew them at the time. That may not have been strictly true, but the family had money.

Mary Magdelina — "Lena" to her friends — became pregnant shortly after the August, 1911 wedding and gave birth to a daughter in May of 1912. They named her Florence Katharine, but unfortunately, she became ill and died before her third birthday.

"He had strong parents," John Mitby says of Alex Jr., and one suspects that kind of enormous tragedy can either strengthen your bond or sap it completely.

In any case, they determined to try again and on March 3, 1914, Alexander John Jordan was born in Madison. As a boy, Alex attended St. James Elementary School where he clashed with the nuns.

"The Notre Dame nuns had a go at it with Alex," is the way John Korb puts it. Korb's mother, Esther, was a good friend of Alex's mother, Lena. Lena was a devoutly

Baby photo of Florence

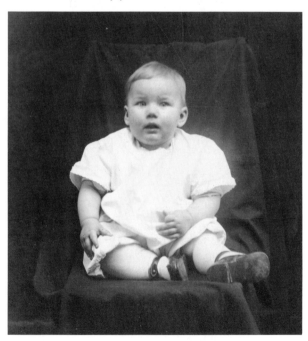

Baby photo of Alex
Photos provided by Jennie Olson

The Jordan family in front of their stately home. Photo provided by Jennie Olson.

Catholic woman, a devotion not shared by her husband, nor, as he grew, by her son.

As a boy, Korb recalls Lena Jordan embracing his mother and saying, "Oh, Esther, the two greatest thorns in my side are my two Alexes."

The Jordans moved around a bit when Alex was a boy. They lived on Brittingham Place in Madison, and then Ely Place, where their home was adjacent to one designed by Frank Lloyd Wright.

"They lived right behind it," Korb says. "That's where some of Alex's inspiration would come. He used to study that house."

One classmate, in an interview with St. Norbert

Alex's Senior High School Picture. Photo provided by Jennie Olson.

College's <u>Knight</u> <u>Life</u> magazine, recalled the youthful Alex as "a boy full of fun and life with a high sense of adventure, creativity and a knowledge and love of electronic gadgets."

It was to St. Norbert's High School (now known as Abbott Pennings), an adjunct to the DePere, Wisconsin college, that Alex Jordan went in 1929. Lena probably favored the move because of the religious instruction Alex would receive at St. Norbert's.

His interests, however, lay elsewhere, and somewhat — as Korb noted — presaged the passion for architecture and entertainment that was to become his obsession. He spent a lot of time making sketches and models of ships and houses.

"He had amazing dexterity with his hands," Sid Boyum recalled. "Alex could work with his fingers like nobody I've ever known."

In the Knight Life article, it was also revealed that young Alex's mind was as agile as his fingers, and that this occasionally led him into pranks.

The Reverend Joseph Regan, a high school classmate, described for the magazine a card trick he and Jordan used to play on younger students.

"The boys all looked up to us because we were older and supposed to set the example," Father Regan said. "We would invite them (younger students) up to our room, and Alex would amaze them with his ability to read their minds."

Alex would pick a card from the deck, not looking at it, and hold it face out for the others to see. He would look deeply into the other students' faces. He was, he said, reading their minds.

When he guessed the correct card, Father Regan recalled, "Oh my, but they were amazed." What the astonished young students didn't know, Father Regan said, is that "I was up in the attic. Looking through a hole in the ceiling, I would signal what the card was to Alex on one of his electronic gadgets. To this day, I think some of those boys still think Alex read their minds."

Alex also played football at St. Norbert's, his powerful frame having been shaped for the sport while working summers for Alex Sr., who, possibly influenced by Lena's developer father, had expanded out of the meat business into real estate.

The elder Jordan's most ambitious project was to build a rooming house for female students at the University of Wisconsin. Eventually called the Villa Maria, it was constructed on Howard Place off Langdon Street on campus.

According to House of Alex, an unauthorized and decidedly unsympathetic portrait of the Jordans written by Madison newspaper reporter Marv Balousek, Alex Sr. obtained a $60,000 loan to begin building. The name — Villa Maria — was a nod to Lena and her deep religious beliefs.

The family may have found itself overextended. Sid Boyum, who met Alex Jr. about this time, visited often

Alex's football team. Jordan is located in the second row, fourth from the left. Photo provided by Jennie Olson.

and recalled the scene in an interview for this book.

"We were buddies," Boyum said of he and young Alex. "We grew up together. In the old days, when I met Alex, I'd go up there and they were so poor — I was, too. They'd be sitting on piles of dirt in the Villa Maria. The old man would work Alex day and night."

"Alex didn't have it easy early in his life," John Mitby says. "He had to figure out a way to survive. He didn't have much. People have suggested he had (wealth) all his life. This was a very poor man for a long, long period of time."

The physical labor strengthened Alex for football, Boyum felt, but it may also have bred resentment.

"Alex plastered the whole inside of the Villa Maria," Boyum said. "He put in the whole heating system. I remember him laying heating pipes in the basement. It developed his arms and shoulders for football, but his legs were thin. He was a barrel on two sticks."

Perhaps, but Jordan played fullback and at well over 200 pounds was an imposing ball carrier.

Boyum recalled that Alex "broke most of his fingers playing football," likely the first in a series of physical injuries, accidents and ailments that plagued the robust Jordan at various stages of his life.

Many years later, Tom Kupsh would recall Jordan, who was having trouble walking, slipping while coming down to visit his workshop, and reacting with annoyance verging on bitterness that his body had betrayed him. "This was a very proud person," Kupsh says. "He didn't want to admit his body was failing him. He wanted to be a lot younger. He wanted to be more fit."

That was some time in the future, of course. After graduating from St. Norbert's High School, and working that summer in Madison, Jordan returned to St. Norbert's, this time to attend the college. But his heart wasn't in it. He lasted "probably a year" — as he noted in one of his rare interviews — and then returned to Madison.

He enrolled at the UW in pre-med classes, most likely at his mother's urging. After witnessing his first operation, however, he knew the medical field wasn't for him. For a while he drove a cab in Madison. As often happens with people in their late teens and early 20s, Jordan was restless. He felt he had some important contribution to make, but what?

Boyum recalled that it was about this time that he and Alex embarked on some enterprises designed to turn a fast dollar. Some were harmless, others less so — another example of a fertile mind in need of a direction in which to apply itself. That, of course, would come soon enough.

In the meantime, Jordan and Boyum hit on a plan to use an infrared camera to take pictures of people's houses. Presumably they would be surprised and impressed by the effect and would want to purchase the photo.

"It looked like snow on the ground," Boyum recalled. "Everything green turned white (when shot with the infrared). I'd go out and try to sell them for $2 a piece, but I'd always take a dollar."

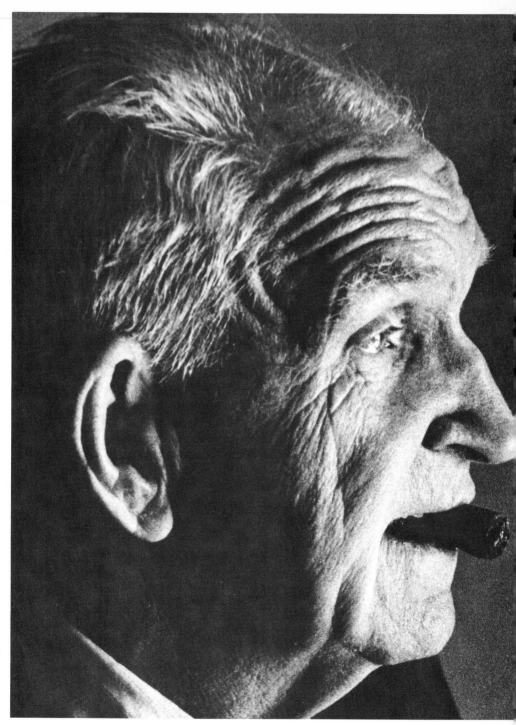

Cigars were the trademark of the eccentric Sid Boyum. Photo by Rich Rygh of The Capital Times, Madison.

"It was legitimate," Boyum recalled with a chuckle. "Alex was a damn good photographer. He turned some beautiful stuff out."

Another time — this was, you'll recall, in the Depression of the 1930s — Boyum approached his friend with an idea.

"Alex," Boyum said, "the big thing now is runs in women's stockings."

"You're right," Jordan replied.

Boyum said, "Why don't we develop a solution that will stop them, put it in a box, and sell it to women?"

The two repaired to the basement, and, using a teaspoon of cement in water, came up with a solution that at one point was netting them $50 a day.

Did it really work? "Cement does stop runs," Boyum said, somewhat cryptically.

Yet another time the pair sold fancy cheeses. "I ran into a guy at the liquor store," Boyum said, "who had a lot of imported cheeses in boxes for $10 a piece. I told Alex we were getting out of the photo business and into the cheese business."

They sold the cheese at fraternity and sorority houses, encouraging the kids to mail the cheeses home to the family. The plan derailed when it developed the cheese did not travel well.

Later the roguish friends traveled in a car that Alex claimed had belonged to the movie star, Ann Sheridan. The truth, Boyum said, was that "Alex rebuilt that in the back yard."

Boyum continued, "People thought it was a Cadillac, but it was a built-over Packard with a rumble seat. "We'd drive around town and everyone would look at it. Alex would say it had belonged to a movie star. He liked Ann Sheridan, so he said, 'We'll tell them we bought it out in Hollywood and that Ann Sheridan owned it.' "

Sid Boyum — photographer, fisherman, and all-purpose eccentric (at the time of his death, he lived alone in Madison with dozens of cats) — was also friends with Alex's father, Alex Sr.

The elder Jordan knew Boyum was also acquainted with a Richland Center, Wisconsin boy who had grown up to become one of the world's greatest and most controversial architects.

Frank Lloyd Wright's Taliesin house, begun near

Spring Green early in this century, is an acknowledged masterpiece. One day Alex Jordan Sr. asked Boyum if he thought Wright, who was at Taliesin, might consent to giving his thoughts on Jordan's Villa Maria design. They bundled up the plans and drove out Highway 14 toward Spring Green.

Wright, of course, was not famous for kindnesses toward his fellow man. He also was not shy about voicing his opinion on any subject.

In his autobiography, An Open Book, film director John Huston, recalled a time in the late 1930s when a mutual friend brought Wright to Huston's home in the San Fernando Valley outside of Los Angeles.

Huston observed, "Wright cut a somewhat theatrical figure with his silver-white mane, worn long for that period, a cape and a big Bohemian Quarter hat."

Huston nervously showed the great man his living room, only to see strong disappointment in Wright's face.

"I don't like high ceilings," Wright said. "I like the sense of shelter that a low ceiling gives. Why do you have high ceilings, Mr. Huston?"

Huston explained that as a tall man — over six feet — he appreciated the space and freedom of a high ceiling.

"Anyone over five-ten is a weed," Wright said.

That may seem a trifle harsh, but it pales in comparison to the reaction generated by Sid Boyum and Alex Jordan Sr. when they called on Wright at the schoolhouse at Taliesin.

"This is Mr. Jordan from Madison," Boyum told Wright. "He's made some plans for a women's rooming house and I think they're pretty nice. Would you look at them?"

Wright took the plans and studied them briefly. He walked to a window and stood looking out.

"I wouldn't hire you to design a cheese case for me, or a chicken coop," Wright said.

"That," Boyum recalled, "was the end of the interview."

Driving home, the elder Jordan was furious. "I'm going to get even with him," Jordan told Boyum. "I'm going to put a Japanese house up out there."

Of course, the world now knows it was not Alex Sr., but his son, Alex Jr., who ended up putting much more than a "Japanese house" in that beautiful area south

Regardless of Frank Lloyd Wright's opinion, Alex Sr. proved his architectural ability with the Villa Maria. Photo provided by Jennie Olson.

of Spring Green known as the Wyoming Valley.

It was Alex Jr. who found Deer Shelter Rock, upon which the House On The Rock now stands, and ironically, although he never met Frank Lloyd Wright, Alex Jr. did invite both Wright's sister and his two sons to the House early in its construction.

John Korb said Jordan related the story to him. "Wright's sister was a frequent visitor," Korb says. "So were both his sons, John and Lloyd. Lloyd helped Alex with a couple of problems in the House in the placement of windows."

That, of course, was still to come. For now, Alex Jordan had finally found a project, and a setting, to fully engage his talents.

3   Breaking Ground

The land is rich in both lore and scenic beauty. A short essay on the region's history, prepared for an early House On The Rock brochure, begins, "Millions of years ago volcanos spewed lava here . . . ."

It goes on to trace other key elements of South Central Wisconsin's past. The ice glaciers obviously pushed around the area, leaving the terrain unglaciated and varied, with rolling hills, deep valleys, thick woods and wildlife.

Indians were likely the first people in the region. The Mound People — metalworking Indians — discovered copper, silver, meteoric iron, flint, quartzite, obsidian and lead. Other Indian cultures included the Winnebagoes, Sauk, Chippewas and perhaps a half dozen more.

French explorers developed a prosperous fur trade with the Indians and were followed by the English. In 1832, the famed Sauk Chief, Blackhawk, was defeated at the Battle of Bad Axe and the land was truly open for European settlers.

The physical beauty of the land exists yet today, and was captured in a 1984 <u>Milwaukee Journal</u> feature.

"Here, the Wisconsin River bends west across Sauk, Iowa, Richland, Grant and Crawford Counties. The river is indolent in this part of the state . . ."

"Blaze-orange snapdragons share the summer hillsides with dairy herds, and a willow grove on a sand island in the river sags in the hazy heat . . . The land

here has character, especially near the Wisconsin and Mississippi Rivers, where white oak, hickory and walnut trees cloak the limestone ridges; where mute, barren bluffs rise like stoic sentinels over wooded valleys, where country roads slither, twist and hump at the geological whims of the area."

One of the most striking geological whims is Deer Shelter Rock, standing 450 feet above the Wyoming Valley and measuring 70 by 200 feet across the top.

When Alex Jordan was a boy, he would visit a grandmother who lived near Spring Green and it was then, while exploring on foot, that he first came across Deer Shelter Rock. He returned as often as possible to picnic, or to simply sit on soft summer days and gaze out toward the Baraboo Bluffs, which on a clear day can be seen some thirty miles in the distance.

"I think every kid wants a place that's his own," Jordan later told Kimberly Clark in an interview. "You know, a retreat or something like that. At first, we used to picnic on the rock. A little steak, a small hibachi . . . a whole gallon of Tom Collins."

By 1945, Jordan had been turned down by the armed forces (because of a heart condition that would haunt him later in life), and he then worked for the Badger Ordnance Works in Baraboo. That year his father, Alex Sr., sold the Villa Maria and began a construction contracting business. Alex Jr. worked for him as well as beginning, in earnest, to try to create something the world had never before seen atop Deer Shelter Rock, south of Spring Green.

One of the first people Alex brought to the rock was Jennie Olson, a lovely young woman he had met in the late '30s and who would become his companion for life.

In a two-hour conversation with this author, Jennie recalled Alex carrying some of the first buckets of mortar and rock from the quarry below to the peak where he would begin building the House. Originally he had a simple tent atop Deer Shelter Rock until a summer storm blew it away. That, and perhaps Frank Lloyd Wright's snub of his father, fueled his desire to create something more substantial.

At 80, Jennie Olson is a keenly aware woman. She spoke fondly of Alex and it was clear that in their more than 50 years together, through good times and bad, they had loved one another and she now missed him very much.

All those years ago, he spoke to her of the great house he wanted to build. Jennie remembers Alex penning his own variation to Don Blanding's poem which depicts the essence of what he was envisioning atop Deer Shelter Rock:

When I have a house ... as I sometime may
I'll suit my dream in every way
It wont be correct or in period style
But oh, I've thought for a long, long while
Of all the corners and all the nooks,
Of all the bookshelves and all the books
The sheepskin divan, the deep soft chairs
And the Chinese rug at the foot of the stairs,
(its an old, old rug from far Chow Wan.
that a chinese princess once walked on)

[The original House On The Rock, which opened in 1960, featured a 17-shelf three-story bookcase.]

My house will stand on a rock on a hill
Overlooking a valley, deep and still
With big tall pines on gaurd nearby
Where the birds can sing and the storm winds cry
A bridge and a stair with lazy curves
Will lead to a door where a great gong serves
As a knocker there like a vibrant drum
to let me know that a friend has come
and the door will squeak as I swing it wide
To welcome you to the cheer inside

The Winter Room, the very first room completed, served as a studio workshop. Photo by G.B. Telfair.

For I'll have good friends who can sit and chat
Or simply sit, when it comes to that,
   In the winter room where the birch logs blaze
   And the smoke rolls up in a wavering haze.
   I'll want a wood box, scarred and rough
   For leaves and bark and fragrant stuff
   Like piney knots and cones and grass;
To throw on the flames when winter comes
And I hope a cricket will stay around
For I love its creaky lonesome sound

Early photo of Jordan's retreat. Photo from the House On The Rock archives.

Many long shelves of wood will hold
my best loved books in leather and gold
while my records will be in a hollow log stand
in a hodge podge mixture close at hand
I'll have on a low wall a rich brocade
that I think the pixies must have made
For the dull gold thread on blues and grays
Weaves a pattern of smoke, or is it haze?
on the hi fi cabinet I'll have a place
For a little switch, and with upturned face
I can watch the ceiling move away
and let in the dawn of another day

The beams of my house will be strong fir wood
That once in a western forest stood
The windows will slant to the rocky ledge
And meet the crag at the very edge
There will be pools in my house with rock and vines
And ceilings of wood with slanted lines
So many trees as you look about
That you'll hardly know if you're in or out
The roof must have an easy dip
To shadowy eaves where the rain can drip
in a damp persistent tuneful way
(its a cheerful sound on a gloomy day))

and I want a shingle loose somewhere
To wail like a banshee in despair
when the wind is high and the storm gods race
and I am snug by my fireplace
I hope a couple of birds will nest
around the house. I'll do my best
to make them happy, so every year
they'll raise their brood of fledglings near.

I'll have a window-seat broad and deep
where I can sprawl to read or sleep
with the windows placed so I can turn
and watch the sunsets blaze and burn
One long thin room will hang in space
and at the end there'll be a place
For a kindly saint as a figurehead
to turn away the thin heights dread
and to bless my house by night and day
and to keep all fearfull things away

In 1985, the 14th room was added to the original House, and it has proven to be one of the House's most remarked-upon features. It would probably be even more so if people knew Alex Jordan had been planning it for 40 years.

The Infinity Room, as it is now called, projects some 218 feet over the Wyoming Valley, with glass walls containing 3,264 windows. This extraordinary room is truly "hanging in space".

And there where the shadows fall I've planned
To have a magnificent Concert-Grand
With polished wood and ivory keys
For wild discordant rhapsodies
discordant
For wailing minor Hindu songs
For Chinese chants and muted gongs
For Carillon bells and lullabies
And moody things that I'll   improvise
To play the long gray dusk away
and bid good bye to another day

One picture I love the best of all
Will hang alone on my study wall
Where the sunsets glow and the moons cold gleam
Will fall on the face and make it seem
That the eyes in the picture are meeting mine,
That the lips are curved in the fine sweet line
Of the + wistful, tender provocative smile
That has stirred my heart for a wondrous while
It's the sketch of a girl who loved too well
To tie me down to that bit of hell
That a dreamer knows when he finds he's held
By the soft strong chains that passion weld

31

All these things I will have about
Not a one could I do without
The white birch trees, and the glass stained blue
The bronze statue of an old Hindu
A nightingale with song to treasure
And Ali Baba jugs of ample measure
a secret   Open Sesame Door
an inlay a pool in the living room floor
and fish with glittery silvery scales
(the kind that grow on mermaids tails)

Pewter and bronze and hammered brass
old carved wood and gleaming glass
Statues and weird candlesticks
aladin lamps with magic wicks
St Francis in a forest bower
Gleaming mirrors   and a tiled shower
all the beautiful useless things
That a dreamers aimless dreaming brings

The perfect "bachelor's nest" — Alex cleaning house. Photo from the House On The Rock archives.

Then when my house is all complete
I'll stretch me out on the window seat
with a favorite book and a cigarette
and a long cool drink and the table set
and I'll look about my bachelor-nest
while the sun goes surfing down the west
and the hot gold light will fall on my face
and make me think of the other place
that I've failed to start ... that I've missed some way
a place that I'd planned to build some day...,
and I'll feel the lure of it drawing me.

I'm sure   I know what the end will be

The House On The Rock. Photo from the House On The Rock archives.

Some dream house! We all have our dreams, yet for most of us, they remain just that — dreams. Alex, however, lived his dreams by turning visions into reality and along with his visions, the dreams and hopes of us all.

Jordan adapted another poem which he later engraved in the mantle in the living room of the House On The Rock . . .

"I hope you will come visit me,
"In the House On The Rock, by the windblown tree;
"For the door opens to views beyond,
"For poet, and artist, and vagabond.
"A cozy chair . . .

Jordan captured the comfort of a warm fire and a breathtaking view. Note the poem above the mantel. Photo from the House On The Rock archives.

The staff at the House On The Rock eventually had to cover the poem because so many visitors stopped to copy it that it was interfering with the flow of traffic through the House.

When Jordan wrote the poem, he was ambitious, for he had a great deal of work still ahead of him.

All the Galena limestone used to build the House, atop Deer Shelter Rock, was from the quarry on the original 200 acre farm. Alex was nicknamed "the Mountain Goat" for he often strapped wicker baskets to his back and carried the necessary stone and mortar up ladders. Due to the increase of curious visitors, Jordan installed a stairway to replace a rope ladder. This stairway worked much the same as a drawbridge. Jordan was able to raise or lower it from controls at the base and the top of the rock.

A 1965 <u>Chicago Tribune Sunday Magazine</u> article noted that the building of the original House required "5,000 tons of limestone" and "5,000 tons of mortar." The electric hoist was installed in 1952. The first room that was completed was a studio workshop, which is now the Winter Room.

This may be a good time to address the question of whether Alex Jordan built the original House by himself. Of course he didn't. The story of Jordan paying the kids who helped him has already been related by Sid Boyum. Others would be given a bottle of whiskey or just a place to relax and party when a hard physical day was done. In an interview with the <u>Wisconsin State Journal</u> in June of 1988, Jordan said of the early construction, "I had helpers. Friends."

Nevertheless, one of the most enduring criticisms of Jordan, in later years, was that he had taken sole credit, both for building the House in the early days, and for creating the artifacts and exhibits that filled it.

There is some validity to the criticism. In his 1971 Kimberly Clark interview, Jordan is quoted as saying, "I worked on it for years pretty much alone. Didn't even have a hoist. Carried up the cement, carried up the sand, carried up the water and timbers. Oh, I was powerful back in those days, you wouldn't believe it. Those were the fun years, those first years . . . I did practically the whole top by myself."

According to Sid Boyum, however, it was Boyum, not Jordan, who came up with the "one man alone" idea and sold it to Alex.

"We got to talking about P.T. Barnum," Boyum recalled. Barnum, of course, was one of the world's most flamboyant, legendary showmen.

"I told him there was no reason he couldn't follow in Barnum's footsteps as a legend," Boyum said. "So I decided to make a legend out of him." Boyum wrote the copy for many early brochures which advanced the idea.

"I set up this legend for Alex that he had done this whole thing," Boyum said, "and he used to ball me out for it. I'd tell people, 'Yeah, he did it all by himself.' Alex would say to me, 'Go out and look at the House. You know how many people worked on it.' "

In the end, probably because it was as the English say, "good for trade," Jordan didn't really try to correct the record. And the fact is the House even today in all its spectacular variety is the product of Jordan's ideas and direction. He had help — but his soul is at the center.

Later on, as he drew on help from a variety of skilled workers, Jordan grew increasingly uneasy about accepting sole credit.

House General Manager Greg Burke recalls, "To my knowledge Alex never came out and said, 'This is my design' about any piece. If things were written, well, he didn't dispute them because he did so few interviews. But he didn't want to take credit for everything."

"He disliked our video (on the House)," Burke continues. "The first time it aired on the property, I sat with him. He wanted it changed. He felt like it said, 'Alex Jordan' way too many times. 'This is everybody's,' he said."

Kupsh offers this perspective: "It is Alex Jordan's place and his attraction. But the place got so big and there was so much stuff that any rational person would say, 'Hey, wait a minute. There must be some people in the back working on this stuff.'"

Back in the early '50s there wasn't all that much to take credit for beyond the view. It was 1952 when Jordan finally got electricity at the fledgling House and by the next year, 1953, he decided he'd better investigate who owned the property and see about leasing it.

The farm, on which Deer Shelter Rock was located, comprised 240 acres and was owned by Oscar Christianson and his wife, Geraldine. The farm had been in the Christianson family since 1880. Oscar's grandfather had immigrated to the area from Norway.

Oscar Christianson's father bought the farm from Oscar's grandfather in 1900. Oscar was born in a house on the property and eventually purchased the farm from his father in 1942. A house that still stands on the property was built in 1945, and a short time later Oscar built a road that leads from Highway 23 back in to the farm.

Jordan struck a deal with the Christiansons in June of 1953. "Whereas," it began, "the said Alex J. Jordan (Jr.) . . . has built one certain house or cottage upon a rock on the farm belonging to the said Oscar Christianson and his wife, Jerry Christianson, and all parties

Aerial View of Christianson Farm. Photograph from the House On The Rock archives.

are desirous of executing a formal written document setting forth the rights of all the parties herein . . ."

In plain English, the deal called for Jordan to pay the Christiansons $7.50 a year for 40 years. Jordan paid the entire amount in advance — $300 — at the time the lease was signed.

In 1955, Geraldine Christianson's brother, Don Martin, originally from nearby Highland, Wisconsin, got out of the service and returned to the area. He began farming with Oscar, his brother-in-law.

Martin recalls seeing Jordan only sporadically at that time. "I didn't know him that well then. He had the rock leased and I was farming. I wasn't around him much. He liked his privacy."

Early photo of Don Martin. Photograph by G.B. Telfair.

Jordan's physicality did make an impression, however. "He was an awesome guy," Martin recalls. "Strong as a bull. He must have weighed 250 pounds."

By the fall of 1956, however, Martin found himself out of a job. The Jordans — with the money coming from Alex Sr. — bought his brother-in-law's farm. Christianson received $12,000 for the 240 acres.

Martin spent about six months driving a truck for someone in the cattle business. Then one day Alex Jordan spoke with Oscar Christianson and mentioned he might be hiring a full-time person to help him out at the House.

Christianson suggested his brother-in-law, Don Martin, and on April 1, 1957, Martin was hired. He would work for Jordan for more than 30 years, becoming in the process an unsung hero of the House On The Rock.

"It was an experience," Martin recalls of the beginning months. "I guess I was more nervous than anything else. I was nothing but a dumb farmer, a greenhorn. The first year I worked with Alex, I had never laid a stone in my life, or done carpentry work. I had never held a skillsaw in my hand."

(Ironically, it was some 15 years later, in October of 1972, when Martin, by then an accomplished carpenter, sustained a serious injury when a saw slipped and cut his thumb to the bone.)

Early on, Jordan was encouraging and set an example by working hard himself. In a sense, Alex, too, was learning on the job.

"Alex didn't really know carpentry," Martin says. "He could lay stone. He was a very good stonemason. That first year we worked side-by-side. I guess I was kind of lucky because Alex was never very fussy. If it wasn't square or plumb it didn't matter. If it had, I'd have been fired the first week. He was more interested in the creative effect than in making the building square."

Late in the fall of 1957 it became evident, in Martin's words, "that there wasn't going to be enough work for me in the winter." Martin was laid off and went back to Highland. But the following spring, on Good Friday, Jordan drove to Highland and asked Martin to come back to work.

"He told me I could stay as long as I wanted," Martin says. "He wasn't going to lay me off again."

Martin believes it was at this time, probably at the urging of his father, that Jordan first began mulling the idea of opening the House to the public and charging admission. "They had plans then to open it up," Martin says. "Why else hire somebody?"

Martin noted the differences between father and son with amusement.

"His dad dressed well," Martin says. "He always wore a white shirt and tie as long as I knew him. Alex never wore a tie. He'd wear the same tan corduroy pants 14 days in a row and his shoes were beat-up. You'd swear he never had a nickel in his life. But if that's what made him happy, who's to say he should have been different?"

40

These photographs of Alex Sr. depict his attitude of "proper attire". White shirt and tie were always appropriate as far as he was concerned. Unlike dad, however, Alex Jr. chose a more casual look. Photos provided by Jennie Olson.

His father, for one. "The first few years they argued like cats and dogs," Martin says. "The old man had the money and Alex had the ideas."

It could make the working situation a little delicate when Alex Sr. stopped by, but Martin remembers both of Jordan's parents fondly.

"His father was a real nice guy," Martin says, "and his mother was wonderful. Alex had the nicest parents a guy could have. Although his mother always told me he had been spoiled since day one. He always got his way."

With the exception of the six months when he was laid off, Martin worked for Alex Jordan for 32 years. Martin and his wife still live in a house on the property

Alex and his mother. Photo provided by Jennie Olson.

and both continue to work for the House On The Rock. He says his relationship with Jordan was a good one.

"He was a nice guy to work for," Martin says. "There were those who wouldn't agree. But I only had one argument with him in 32 years. I don't even remember what started it. But we went around and around for about 10 minutes, and that was it. We did get along. I knew when to walk away. You learned about his good days and bad days."

A workshop (today called the Alex Jordan Creative Center) would eventually be built across Highway 23, but in those early years they used the basement of Martin's house as a workshop.

"It was nice for me," Martin recalls. "I didn't have far to go to work. I also gave Alex a bedroom upstairs that he used for an office."

Perhaps the relationship endured because they respected one another's privacy. Don Martin is the kind of guy who goes into town once a week to church or for a haircut. He has little use for cities and enjoys keeping to himself. His interview for this book was the first time he has spoken publicly about Alex Jordan. As for Jordan, his conviction that one's private life should remain that way is well-documented.

So they had that in common, as well as the House On The Rock. In the first couple of years Martin was there, one large project involved planting. It's hard to believe today, but most of the land between Highway 23 and Deer Shelter Rock was originally an open field.

Jordan and Martin planted 55,000 trees and 55,000 shrubs. They took out a number of old farm fences and tore down the farm buildings — all but the house where Martin still lives.

"The dream for years was to have a tunnel of trees leading to the House," Martin says. Finally they grew so dense that tour buses were getting scratched coming up the driveway, and the trees were cut back.

Inside the House, Martin recalls that one of his first tasks involved putting in one foot by one foot glass windows.

There has been much speculation over the years as to whether blueprints ever existed for the original House. Balousek notes that Jordan "used his expertise at model-building to construct a detailed replica for his father of how the Japanese house would look on the rock."

Whenever Jordan was asked about plans, he'd say "it just gradually evolved" or "all the plans are right here," and then tap the side of his head.

The man in the best position to know, Don Martin, says, "I only saw one set of plans the whole time I was here. They were in his head, and you never knew what was coming one day to the next."

Jordan used to bring cardboard models of his fledgling creation along to dinner with his Madison friends, Homer and Lynn Fieldhouse. In the late '50s, Alex and Jennie Olson came to the Fieldhouse home for dinner nearly every Saturday night.

Homer Fieldhouse had met the Jordans about the time they purchased the farm from the Christiansons. He'd been at a farm auction and picked up some brass and copper kettles. He'd heard of Alex Jordan and what he was doing, so he stopped out and found Alex supervising the planting of trees near the farm house.

"I introduced myself," Fieldhouse says, "and Alex took me up the ladder to the top of the rock where his father was and introduced us. We talked about trees for a while."

Fieldhouse is a landscaper himself, and recalls, "I suggested he transplant some birch trees that were growing on the north slopes of his property, which he did."

He also gave Jordan a copper kettle, which Alex and he carried up from Fieldhouse's truck and which Jordan placed next to a brick fireplace upstairs, where it still stands today.

They became friends — Alex and Jennie and Homer and Lynn Fieldhouse. At the Saturday dinners they would drink and laugh and the talk would eventually drift to Alex's ambitious project atop Deer Shelter Rock.

Homer Fieldhouse recalls, "In the early years, before he named the House, he and Jennie came over to our house every Saturday night for two years. He'd bring some vodka and we'd do a pretty good job on that. The conversation always got around to what he should name the place. He tried out different names, but he kept referring to the House On The Rock and what he should call it. Finally he looked at me one night and said, 'That must be the name. The House On The Rock. That's what we keep calling it.' "

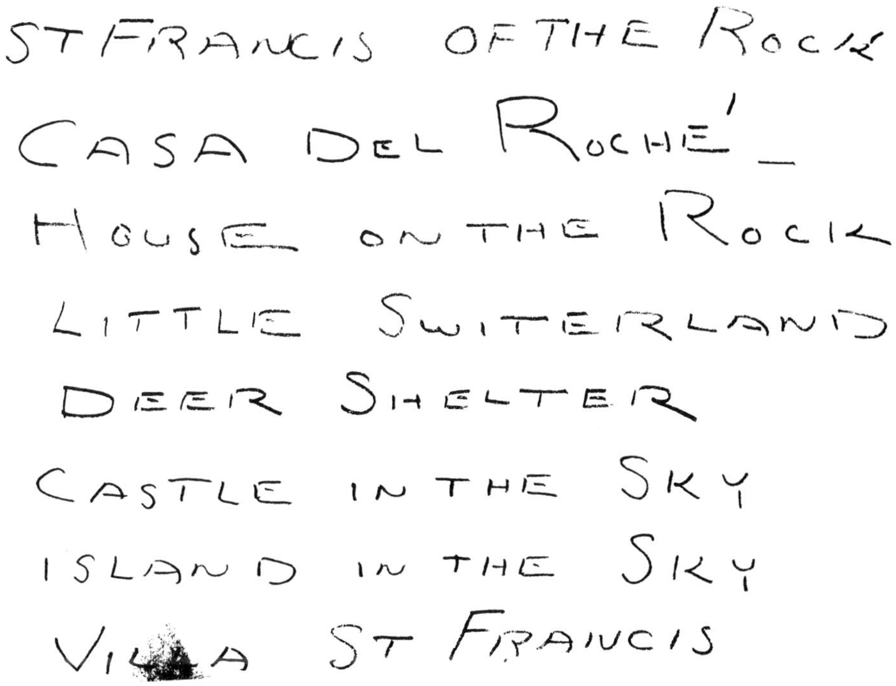

ST FRANCIS OF THE Rock

CASA DEL Roché' _

House on THE Rock

LITTLE Switerland

DEER Shelter

Castle in the Sky

ISLAND in the Sky

Villa ST Francis

As taken from his sketchbook, Alex penned possible names for his retreat. From the House On The Rock archives.

"And that," Fieldhouse concludes, "became the name."

By the summer of 1959, the original House — at least to a visitor's eye — appeared finished. Harry Johnson, a Madison <u>Capital Times</u> reporter, came out and was bowled over and wrote what seems to have been the first article done on the House On The Rock.

Readers today will not be surprised to learn that while Johnson did interview Alex Jordan, calling him an "artist and sculptor as well as a worker in stone and wood," the creator of the House asked if the reporter would please "write about the House and not about the man."

Johnson concentrated on the House, but he couldn't resist comparing Jordan to the Italian architect Fillippo Brunelleschi, "who got the job of building the first dome of its kind 135 feet above the walls of an unfinished cathedral in his native Florence. It took him 14 years (1420-1434)."

By 1959, Jordan had been at work 15 years, and told Johnson, "I consider the job only half done." As we now know, Jordan was never really "done" with the House On The Rock. He was still planning future exhibits at the time of his death.

By the summer of 1959, however, and the visit of Capital Times reporter Harry Johnson, much of the original House was in place. Johnson was more than a little impressed, and it's worth quoting his story at some length:

"Once you catch your breath, the first reaction to this house is: 'Unusual!' 'Out of this world!'

"But stay a while and you'll realize it's a thing of beauty, too.

"And the view . . .

"A small bridge leads from the living room to an island facing Percussion Rock (also chimney-shaped, nearby Percussion Rock is smaller than the 100,000-ton Deer Shelter Rock) looks down on Wyoming Valley and towards the distant Baraboo Bluffs.

"The sundeck on the roof offers an unsurpassed view to the northwest towards Highland and Clyde with the Larson farm buildings looking like toy structures down below.

G.B. Telfair's wife and son enjoy the spectacular view from the sundeck. Photo by G.B. Telfair.

Bell Gallery. Photo from the House On The Rock archives.

"The original living room has a huge fireplace and next to it is a studio with a skylight that automatically opens and shuts.

"This raised-level-room contains the television and the hi-fi.

"Beyond the studio is the winter room with another fireplace, an electric oven and hotplates built into the rocks.

"The large patio consists of many parts.

"There's the garden area with its growing trees and plants and the raised shelter house with a large fireplace and oven used for 'cook outs'.

"Steps lead to the sun deck that will soon be screened in and transformed into a roof garden.

"The entrance to the house is a narrow passageway called the 'bell gallery' that will some day contain thirty large metal bells . . .

"There are pools with changing colored lights and a waterfall cascading down over the rocks into the sheltered area of the patio."

Johnson was bewitched, and before long, many others would be too.

4 "I Hope You Will Come and Visit Me"

Alex Jordan never had a problem with people coming to see his creation.

The entire time Alex was building the House On The Rock, he allowed curious visitors to come up and take a look at what he was building. Often he or his father would act as tour guide. Weekend parties were quite common, for Alex often entertained fellow artists and Madison friends. As the House started to take shape, Alex often rented it out for weekends. Some people in Madison circles still speak of the great times they had in the original House.

"He especially had parties around the Fourth of July," Lynn Fieldhouse recalls. "Those were the only nights he stayed at the House overnight. He'd have a group of good friends — maybe 15 or 20 — and we'd stay up all night partying. It was marvelous."

She recalls in those years the House windows were clear glass. "At that time you could look over the vistas and it was just gorgeous, especially in the fall."

In his 1971 interview with Kimberly Clark, Jordan recalled his decision to open the House to the public in the summer of 1960.

"Word got out that there was something to see out here, and people began coming around," Jordan said. "They'd holler up, 'Can we see your place?' One day we were picnicking and I said, 'By golly, I'm going to charge those folks 50 cents a piece.' And you know, they paid gladly. Thanked me even more when they left. We drank real Scotch that night!"

To those who knew Jordan and his colorful vocabulary, it is doubtful he said precisely, "by golly." But the good-natured decision to go public, as detailed to Kimberly-Clark, does seem in keeping with a man who would write a poem including the line, "I hope you will come and visit me / In the House On The Rock by the windblown tree."

Certainly it is more in keeping than the grumpy tale reporter Steven Hannah was told when he encountered Jordan at the House On The Rock in 1975. Hannah was hoping to sell a piece to the Milwaukee Journal, and, well, you know by now how Jordan felt about reporters.

Hannah met Jordan in the parking lot where Jordan was unloading some hand-woven religious silks he'd purchased that morning. The reporter asked about taking his picture, which Jordan appreciated as much as someone lifting his wallet.

He declined to be photographed, but he did stop to speak for a minute.

"I started out to build a studio," Jordan said. "A weekender. I never intended to live here. Then it sort of snowballed. I guess you could say I backed into it."

Hannah then asked about going public. "Well, for one thing, I needed money," Jordan said. "Then, after the studio was finished, people would come around and ask to see it. Goddamn Sunday gawkers — you know, the country's full of them. I decided if they wanted to see the place so badly, they could pay. I figured it would discourage them. It didn't."

Jordan continued, "The first day we opened this place to the public, we made $15. That night we drank Scotch."

Perhaps the truth resides somewhere between the Kimberly-Clark and Milwaukee Journal interviews. For there was some ambivalence in Alex Jordan's decision to begin charging admission to see his creation. He would be gaining something but also giving something up.

There is this, too: Throughout his life, Alex had chafed under the forceful personality of his father, dating back to the days of the building of the Villa Maria. Alex Sr. was applying increasing pressure to open the House — and to begin charging. The elder

Jordan wanted to see some return on his investment, while Alex, in Sid Boyum's words, "never really cared that much about money."

"I'd guess it was his father's decision," Homer Fieldhouse says. "Alex fought it for a year or two. His father saw all the money going into this place, and to what end? By that time Alex was really building up there."

Fieldhouse's wife, Lynn, concurs and recalls a time just prior to the opening when they visited Jordan out at the House.

"You see, before it was opened, it was a very personal thing with Alex," Lynn Fieldhouse says. "At the time his father was pushing him to open it, he wasn't sure he wanted to. We were out there one day talking about it, and he was angry."

Alex had a bunch of change in his pocket, she recalls, and he took the coins and slung them into the woods.

"His father was so worried about money," Lynn Fieldhouse says. "He said his father had told him he couldn't be putting all that money into it without getting something out of it. So there were a couple of things tugging at Alex. On one level he wanted to keep it personal. On the other he knew that wasn't feasible."

It may not have taken Alex long to warm up to the idea, for as Lynn Fieldhouse says, "Once he did turn it over to the public, and it got going, it gave him his chance to create even more and further his ideas." That would have been impossible without the income from visitors.

There are conflicting emotions and levels of ambiguity in most, if not all, father-son relationships. That was certainly true of Alex Jordan and his father, particularly where the House On The Rock was concerned. As Don Martin noted, "His father had the money and Alex had the ideas."

It could be that Alex never really put those feelings to rest, for driving one day with Sid Boyum, years later — long after his father's death — Alex blurted out, "I think I may buy some land near Mazomanie. There's a nice spot there on a bluff."

"What for?" Boyum asked.

"I'll build another house on it," Alex replied. "That'll be mine. My dad won't have a thing to do with it."

He never did that, of course. In the cool light

of hindsight, both Alex Jordan's immense achievement with the House On The Rock, as well as his father's early financial contribution, seem proportional and secure.

Neither Jordan could have been sure — or even dared to dream — of how the public would react to the opening of the House. Because of all it has become, picturing the House as it was in 1960, when people first began paying their 50 cents to tour it, is not an easy task.

"Each room sort of dictated the flow of the next room," John Korb says. "The first room was the bell gallery, then the winter room, living room, garden room, patio room, contemplation room, banquet room, tea room, and ultimately the music room and observation deck. That was basically completed by late 1960."

The early House reflected Jordan's easy male swagger. Basic rough timbers accentuated the very masculine decor. Additional revenue, generated by the increased number of visitors, allowed Alex to add exquisite collections of bronzes, stained glass lamps and windows, rosewood root carvings, as well as porcelain cinnabar. With all these additions, he certainly was establishing himself as a collector of international acclaim.

As Lynn Fieldhouse noted earlier, one feature of the early House was the clear windows which allowed a stunning view of the Wyoming Valley. At some point later, perhaps because it allowed him to better experiment with lighting, Jordan effectively closed the windows with blue shading. Some people thought it a good idea, others were less enthusiastic. It is likely the single largest change in the original main House from the early years.

The introduction of canted windows truly added to the magnificent view. Because they were designed to project out from the floor to the ceiling, a spectacular view clear down to the forest floor was achieved.

Alex had to work with the natural flow of the rock. His creation complemented nature instead of destroying it, for the trees and ferns remained undisturbed. The House On The Rock began as a retreat where Alex often came to work on his artwork. Many of his original sculpted pieces, such as large casks, are still on display in the House.

Since Alex always appreciated and enjoyed a good fireplace, he built five of them in the original

One of the five fireplaces in the original House On The Rock. Photo from the House On The Rock archives.

House alone. To highlight the natural setting he had created, he added four pools and kept them sparkling with recirculating water.

It is only after touring the main House with its complex design offering constant surprises — low ceilings, towering bookshelves, waterfalls and fireplaces — that one can truly appreciate Jordan's feat of putting all this together <u>without</u> <u>a</u> <u>blueprint</u>. He benefited from self-confidence and the willingness to take a chance.

"Another belief and philosophy Alex maintained was never be afraid to admit an error," Korb observed. "One of his firm beliefs was that it would be a major mistake to adhere to a master plan when building or creating. Often he spoke of architects he knew who

One of Alex's favorite rooms was the Organ Room. Photo by G.B. Telfair.

54

locked themselves in with a master plan and would not consider a change or modified design even when it was evident such a change would yield an improvement. It was not uncommon for Alex to redesign a building or display several times and make major revisions as he went along."

In later years, one of Jordan's most eclectic, controversial and remarked-upon creations would be the Organ Room, opened in 1981. It has been described as bizarre, surreal — fascinating, to be sure. It features organs, of course, as well as spiral staircases, walkways and all manner of electrical equipment.

This was the room which one day led Jordan to say to John Korb, "Korb, this Organ Room is a lot better than you think it is."

Korb replied, "No, Alex, it isn't. Because I think it's your best work to date."

That's of particular significance when you consider that prior to Jordan's commencing work on the Organ Room, he invited Lynn Fieldhouse out to the property for a visit. When she arrived, Alex took her out to a cavernous warehouse. "It was just this vast space," she says.

The space was destined to become the Organ Room.

Lynn Fieldhouse recalls, "He stood there and said, 'Up there this is going to happen, and over there that is going to happen.' I couldn't begin to visualize it. Now that it's finished, it's mindblowing. That was his genius. He saw it in his mind's eye, and then he made it happen."

That summer of 1960, upon first opening to the public, Jordan put a stone marker where the long driveway to the House intersected at Highway 23. That was nearly the extent of the public hoopla that greeted the opening. It's remarkable, given its eventual growth, to realize that over the years Jordan rarely advertised.

In later years, he'd pay $1,000 or so to get into the annual travel book put out by the American Automobile Association. Early on, Don Martin did paint some signs in his front yard that were distributed on main roads, but mostly, as Martin says, "It was word of mouth."

They had something else going for them. The House On The Rock was so unusual that eager reporters were happy to feature it.

Martin laughs, recalling how the money was

G.B. Telfair's son admiring the masonry skills of Jordan's stone marker located at the entrance of the House On The Rock. Photo by G.B. Telfair.

collected that first summer. "Alex's dad more or less took care of it," Martin says. "He was on top of the landing with a bag and people would put 50 cents in it."

Somewhat to their surprise, it added up. "They took in $5,000 the first year and thought they had the world by the tail," Martin says.

The next year — 1961 — they took in $34,000 and a second building, the Gate House, was opened. The Gate House serves as a foyer to the main House, leading as it does to the 375-foot ramp through the treetops that takes visitors to the bell gallery and the House entrance.

The Gate House was built after the House was first opened to the public, and Martin says that began a pattern of construction that never ceased.

"We'd never stop working, even after the House opened," Martin says. "We worked right around everyone. You know, we finished the first story, which then everyone could see, and we'd be up working on the second story. There weren't all that many people at the time. We didn't stop year-round."

Of the Gate House, Martin notes, "Alex wanted a front entrance." It is contemporary, innovative, and un-mistakably masculine — stone walls, fireplaces, and a low ceiling.

Being of the same innovative and contemporary design as the original House, the Gate House was designed as an entryway. The Gate House also provided winter shelter for the caretakers.

Since books were so important to Jordan, he was always careful to include a library whenever necessary. The Gate House is no exception. The Gate House also hosts another of Jordan's favorites — a fireplace. Many people appreciate this room for the real warmth and charm it conveys.

In a 1970 interview with the Wisconsin State Journal, Jordan — who was rarely pinned down on this kind of thing — told reporter Barbara Reinherz that he liked the Gate House best (at least he did at that time).

"The Gate House is my favorite," Jordan said, "although some of the best design work was in the original House. The Gate House was the most planned out, and I like it's fireplace."

Reporter Reinherz went on to observe, "The Gate House fireplace encloses a staircase which reaches the upper oven area behind and above the huge pots."

In the first years after the opening of the Gate House, visitors had the opportunity to tour the Water Garden. Since Alex was such an animal lover, the Water Garden served as a haven for all types of waterfowl. Chipmunks, badgers, woodchucks, raccoons, and even skunks could also be found here. Peacocks would seek shelter under a weeping willow on an island in the very center of the garden. The highlight of the Water Garden was a 60-foot wide waterfall. This area has since been turned into refreshment gardens, due largely to the feuds between the waterfowl and the other animals.

Since Alex appreciated and enjoyed art, he built an Artist's Studio for resident artists to display and sell their work. In fact, even today this same tradition is

Jordan takes time out to relax in front of the Gate House Fireplace. Photo from the House On The Rock archives.

continued in the House On The Rock Village Shops.

That would come soon enough, but for now, with the Gate House opened and word of the House's splendor getting out, it was time to get serious about business.

It was about that time the House On The Rock took on someone it sorely needed, Gladys Walsh. She was an extraordinary woman who would do the books and handle the voluminous business correspondence for the House On The Rock for over 20 years. She would be given a place on the House Board of Directors in 1963, shortly after it incorporated.

Gladys Walsh explained to Balousek, "When I started, he (Alex) would bring me money at night and sometimes I had to separate the denominations. It took a while. In the morning, I had a special money belt to bring the money to the bank. Later, it got very big and he started depositing the money in Dodgeville, and they would send me a statement of how much was deposited."

Who was Gladys Walsh? In her two decades with Alex Jordan, she was his woman Friday, if not his right arm. Her correspondence went out nationwide to an eclectic network of suppliers, curious collectors, government regulatory agencies, artists looking to exhibit their wares, teachers seeking tours for their classes — literally tens of thousands of letters over the years.

Gladys Walsh was Jordan's buffer to the public; she could both reign in his creative instincts when they threatened the House's financial security, as well as perform the mundane financial tasks that allowed him the time and freedom to be creative.

Don Martin feels Gladys Walsh is one of the real heroes of the House On The Rock story, and it's easy to see why. A small woman, she was a pillar of strength. When Alex Jordan suffered a near-fatal traffic accident in 1972, he instructed the Iowa County sheriff to call Gladys and ask her to meet him at the hospital.

In truth, Walsh had begun her association with the Jordans while working for Alex Sr. More precisely, she was living at the Villa Maria when Alex Sr. hired her to help in collecting the rents and handling some of the paperwork.

She had a rich history even prior to that time. Gladys Walsh's family came from Ireland. Her paternal grandfather was born there and immigrated to Wisconsin in 1859, settling in Reedsburg. On her mother's side (her mother's maiden name was Allen) there was a relation to the Revolutionary War hero, Ethan Allen.

Gladys was born in Loyal, Wisconsin, right at the turn of the 20th Century. She attended St. Benedict's Academy for Girls in Minnesota, then Eau Claire State College, and eventually taught school for a time in a country schoolhouse near Prairie du Sac.

In the 1920s she moved to Madison, studying to be a secretary at the Madison Business College and proofreading for the Capital Times newspaper. In 1923, she

Gladys Walsh receives commendation as "the People's Lobbyist".
Photo courtesy of Capital Times, Madison.

began a five-year stint as a legal secretary to Wisconsin Attorney General, Herman Ekern.

Walsh later said Ekern taught her law and the importance of writing good bills — it was a primer on the legislative process — and it had a profound effect on her.

For close to 50 years, Walsh would take an intense interest in the Wisconsin Legislature, earning the sobriquet "the people's lobbyist" and sometimes ruffling the feathers of the self-esteemed politicians who wondered who this diminutive, but outspoken, woman might be.

She testified more than 1,000 times in front of various

committees, always beginning, "As a citizen of Wisconsin, and in my own behalf, I respectfully petition . . ."

She favored diversity and fought against the consolidation of power in all arenas. She was a vocal advocate of women's rights, a feminist before anyone knew the word. Walsh's first Legislative appearance in 1931 was to ask for the repeal of a law saying only men could work in the Legislature.

This side career — though that hardly does it justice — culminated in 1971 when the State Senate passed a resolution honoring Gladys Walsh for her "sincere, vigorous and continuing interest in the laws and government of this state . . . (she has been) a people's lobbyist, a defender of women's rights and opponent of undeclared wars long before her petitions became popular rallying points."

In the Senate chamber, Walsh responded, "It is a privilege I shall remember all my life. I have pleaded that the merits of bills be considered without regard to party affiliation. You men represent your district, but you also represent all the people of this state."

In 1976, at the age of 77, Gladys Walsh embarked on a new venture, as a published poet. She described her volume of 60 poems, titled A Basket of Sculptured Thoughts, as "pounding, belting thoughts discussing problems of working, living and eternity and restful pictures of the beauties of nature."

She handled the House On The Rock correspondence in a way that was both business-like and friendly. Her May, 1970, response to C.S. Schneider of Wauwatosa, who was hoping to take advantage of the House's invitation to artists to display their wares at the House On The Rock, is a good example:

"Thank you for your letter," Walsh wrote, advising you would like to exhibit your art works of handcrafted sterling of original design and jewelry at the House On The Rock. You have a very impressive list of awards and places where you have exhibited. It is interesting to know of your interest in craftsmanship. Mr. Jordan wishes you to know you will be very welcome to come and exhibit your works at the House On The Rock."

It says a lot that Jordan could attract a woman of Walsh's caliber to help him at the House — and that she would remain for two decades. It's even more remarkable when you consider Alex had little or no interest in politics.

61

Art Donaldson, who bought the House from Jordan and became close to him in the years leading up to the sale, recalled having long talks with Alex about a variety of subjects, though rarely politics. When the subject came up, Jordan would grunt and say that it didn't matter. Donaldson would later laugh and say Alex might have had a point.

In any case, Jordan always had other fish to fry, particularly by 1962, as his creation atop Deer Shelter Rock began to catch the public's imagination.

One big boost came early in 1962 when Wisconsin Trails publisher Howard Mead came out to prepare a lengthy, illustrated piece for his spring 1962 issue (the magazine was then called Wisconsin Tales and Trails).

Mead was impressed by many aspects of the House, though he dwelled on Jordan's use of and affection for Oriental artifacts.

"Often this effect is heightened by the architecture itself," Mead wrote, "or by hanging Japanese lanterns. Sometimes Jordan's own sculptures — solemn Buddhas, Ming trees, and Japanese lamps, beautiful in their simplicity — provide the Oriental effect. His pottery, like the four foot high, narrow-throated pots, while not Oriental in appearance, do compliment the House with their massive size and bold form."

Mead ended his story by telling his readers what they could expect new at the House in 1962. Through the years, there has always been something, which explains why some people have returned 10 or 20 or 30 times to the House.

In the spring of 1962, Mead noted that "Jordan had opened an extensive five room addition for the first time . . . With the new addition, the House On The Rock has grown from one story to what is to be its extreme height. The old rooftop sundeck has become an art gallery, with circular stairs reaching to the new deck directly above.

"The gallery, which will display the arts and crafts of the area artists, is a vast dramatic room. One entire wall is fireplace and slicing through a corner is the new elevator shaft shaped library, rising three stories from the Patio below.

"Then, branching off the gallery, on different levels, is the Tea House, Jordan's ultimate in the Oriental, and two snug rooms each dominated by fireplaces long enough to burn half an oak. Amazingly, as in the past, each new room maintains a unity of character with the rest of the House, while still housing its own distinctive personality."

Mead also noted that new in 1962 would be "the thunderous sound of 'the world's largest wind chimes,' which Jordan made and tuned recently. The bamboo chime is about four feet long and four inches thick, while the smallest is over ten inches long. In a good wind, these monster chimes really reverberate."

Finally, Jordan titillated Mead with an idea for the future. He told him about the Infinity Room.

"Since there is no more rock to build on," Mead noted, "and since Jordan feels to build higher would destroy the proportion of his House, the only place to go is out into space. The Infinity Room will be canti-levered from the living room out across the island rock observation platform and then seventy-five feet beyond, over the valley."

Mead was skeptical it could ever be done, but he also knew Alex Jordan well enough not to rule anything out.

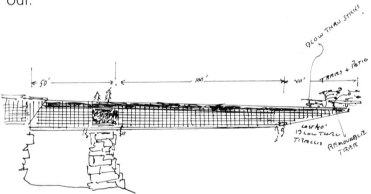

Original drawing from Alex's sketch book. Taken from the House On The Rock archives.

"When you look at the Infinity Room sketches," Mead concluded, "your first reaction is that it can't be done. Your second, if it can, you'll never catch me out there. But then for seventeen years people have been saying that the House On The Rock couldn't be done and Alex Jordan has had an astonishing record of pro-ving them wrong."

Twenty-three years later, Jordan astonished them again. The Infinity Room opened to the public.

5 Growth and Mortality

The meeting was held August 4, 1962 at the Jordan residence in Madison. It was the first board meeting of the newly incorporated House On The Rock. Over the years all subsequent board meetings would be held there.

According to John Korb, the Jordans — Alex Sr., Alex Jr. and Lena — moved shortly after the death of Alex Sr.'s brother, Anton.

Alex Jr. lived there until his death in 1989. Neil Hanson, a House On The Rock employee, describes the home in his talk to groups touring the Alex Jordan Creative Center, which opened at the House after Jordan's death.

"His bedroom reminded me of a 'Leave It to Beaver' rerun," Hanson says. "It had the old, smaller bed with a desk and a lifetime collection of artifacts. He built models all his life, and his home was full of them. It appeared that he would, at times, dump the parts to several models into a box, mix them up, and create something new out of those miscellaneous parts."

Homer and Lynn Fieldhouse recall visiting Alex and Jennie Olson often at Jennie's small Madison apartment in the late 1950s and '60s, and always Alex would have models of two or three projects in the works, sometimes floor to ceiling and dominating the limited space.

The meeting on August 4, 1962, was for business, not creative reasons. Alex Sr. was 77 years old, and he and Lena had celebrated their golden wedding anniversary almost exactly a year earlier in a big bash at the House On The Rock. The time had come to get their affairs in order, to establish the House as a corporation.

The meeting at Alex's house began at 7:30 p.m. Madison attorney, Richard Callaway — today a Dane County Circuit Judge — called the meeting to order. It was decided the officers of the new corporation would be Alex Sr., chairman; his wife, Lena, vice-president; and Alex Jr., secretary. They each received 125 shares of stock in the corporation. Callaway was named assistant secretary.

A decision was also made to open an account with the American Exchange Bank in Madison. All three Jordans were authorized to write checks on the account.

The account was destined to grow dramatically in the 1960s. The income generated by the House On The Rock during that first decade was close to a million dollars earned, but there were expenses. As he would do thoughout his life, Alex Jr. poured much of the money back into the House.

In December of 1964, the Jordans bought more land. The board authorized the purchase of the nearby Reuben Gullick farm for $10,000; ten months later they resolved to buy the Lawrence Waddell farm for $24,500.

To be safe, in June of 1964, the House On The Rock established a line of credit with the American Exchange Bank for $30,000; by 1975, that grew to $250,000.

It was a good thing they incorporated when they did. On June 10, 1963, Alex Sr. died, leaving both his share of the House On The Rock and his Madison real estate holdings to Lena.

The House Board met three months later, on September 14, 1963. Alex made a motion that his mother be made president of the corporation, and that her younger sister, Alex's aunt, Katherine Schmelzer, be vice-president. He also moved that Katherine's son, the Rev. Linus Schmelzer, be appointed to the House On The Rock board of directors, along with Gladys Walsh.

Six months later, in March of 1964, Alex Jordan undertook one of the most unusual adventures of his life. He spent a month in New York City helping prepare the Wisconsin pavilion for the World's Fair that was to open in June.

It was unusual because Jordan disliked traveling with an unnatural passion.

"He wouldn't stay overnight in a motel for anything," Don Martin says.

Martin recalls a buying trip Alex made to St. Louis. He drove down, made his purchase, loaded the truck and drove back. He once did the same thing on a trip to California.

"What did you do in California?" Martin asked.

"Nothing," Jordan replied. "I came back. Jennie had supper on."

Sid Boyum recalled a time when Jordan flew to London, England and returned the very next day. He said to Boyum, "If anyone asks you, you can tell them I've been to Europe."

Art Donaldson recalls a conversation he had with Jordan in which Alex asked him if he liked to travel. Donaldson replied that he liked it a lot. "I did all that when I was younger," Jordan said. "Fancy cars, travel. I got it out of my system."

Late in Jordan's life, Donaldson was talking to him one day when Alex brought up the famous Hearst Castle at San Simeon in California.

"I'd like to see that," Jordan said.

"You know, Alex," Donaldson said, "you're in a position where you could charter a plane out there if you wanted to visit it."

"I don't want to go out there," Jordan said.

As it happened, Donaldson was making a trip to California. "I'll make a video for you," Donaldson said. He said he'd try to tape inside, in order to get a feeling for the grandeur of Hearst's creation.

"I don't want to see that junk!" Jordan said. "I want to see the parking lots and how they handle the people."

So Donaldson made a video of the traffic flow and brought it back from California. He watched it with Alex and Jennie. When it was over, Donaldson asked Jordan what he thought.

"Interesting," Jordan said.

Lynn Fieldhouse has an idea why Jordan, despite his antipathy toward travel, agreed to go to the World's Fair in New York. The Walt Disney Company was planning to unveil a new exhibit at the fair — a lifesize mannequin of Abraham Lincoln that moved and included a barking dog.

Visitors enjoy the two animated figures, featured in the Mikado. Photo by G.B. Telfair.

"Alex was always interested in automation and animation," Lynn Fieldhouse says. "He'd had mechanical toys as a boy and that kind of thing just always fascinated him. Not being a traveler, it really surprised me when he went to New York, but it was in part to see Lincoln."

She thinks Disney's Lincoln may well have planted the seed in Jordan for eventual House On The Rock exhibits such as the Mikado music machine — an Oriental extravaganza featuring moving figures (including a Japanese gentleman playing the kettle drum) and organ music, located in the Music of Yesterday collection that opened at the House in 1974.

It was Lynn's husband, Homer Fieldhouse, who recruited Jordan for the '64 World's Fair. Wisconsin's Lieutenant Governor, Jack Olson, was in charge of hiring people to prepare the Wisconsin exhibit. He first hired Fieldhouse to do the landscaping outside the pavilion, then also asked him to construct a waterfall inside.

"I approached Alex to help me do the interior of the pavilion — to take charge of the waterfall construction," Fieldhouse recalls.

The first thing Jordan did upon signing on was volunteer to have some birch trees from the House On The Rock transplanted out to the exhibit. Like any project that truly captivated his interest, Jordan approached this one with gusto.

Fieldhouse and Jordan drove out to New York in Fieldhouse's car. A third man accompanied them — Edgar Hellum, from Pendarvis House in Mineral Point, who had a good friend in Manhattan and wanted to go along.

Jordan's initial reaction to New York City was, in Fieldhouse's estimation, "quite negative". For one thing, he didn't look remotely like a city slicker.

"Alex and I wore work clothes and work boots," Fieldhouse recalls. "We looked like bumpkins but, you know, we were out there to work. Our landscape guy looked better than we did."

Which wasn't really a problem until one night when Hellum's Manhattan friend, who turned out to be a wealthy, blue-blooded architect, invited the three visitors to dinner at a swank East Coast restaurant.

Fieldhouse recalls, "The gentleman had met Alex and he told Edgar that Alex had to have a suit." Fieldhouse isn't sure why his own lack of tailoring wasn't mentioned — perhaps because Alex was such an imposing physical presence.

"He said Alex couldn't go in his baggy corduroys with the pockets in his jacket ripped out," Fieldhouse says. "He deemed that Alex should be taken down to Brooks Brothers to buy a suit."

They went to Brooks Brothers, and a suit was acquired. Today one of the most widely-circulated pictures of the photo-shy Jordan shows him smiling into the camera while wearing what looks to be a wool suit complete with vest and necktie. That's the suit he bought in New York.

A handsomely attired Jordan in New York for the World's Fair. Photo from the House On The Rock archives.

"It's the one picture of him that looks kind of official," Lynn Fieldhouse says.

Jordan's defiance of propriety, and his total lack of interest in social climbing, were lifelong traits, and admirable in their way. Had he chosen to, Jordan could have moved in elite, monied circles, and joined country clubs. It simply never appealed to him.

John Korb recalls that even at his parents' 50th anniversary party, when he threw them a big bash at the House On The Rock which attracted all kinds of movers and shakers, Alex moved quietly around the fringes of the party, happy for them but somehow distant.

The truth is, he was most comfortable with and preferred the company of Jennie or a few close friends. Better yet, he could be out at the House by himself, playing out new exhibits and ideas in his mind.

On the second day of their New York trip, Fieldhouse and Jordan decided the waterfall in the Wisconsin pavilion needed boulders. They drove out on Long Island, but as Fieldhouse recalls, "We weren't very happy with what we could find."

An interior decorator friend had tipped them on an artist in Oregon who did terrific fiberglass rocks. They wound up buying them from him, and they worked pretty well.

They made at least one ill-advised sojourn into New York nightlife. They decided to take Fieldhouse's car into Greenwich Village, where Homer said he knew of a good restaurant. On their way to the restaurant, their car passed a friend from the fair and Fieldhouse waved for him to stop. He rolled down the window and chatted with the man. Jordan put up with this for all of 30 seconds and then inquired in a loud voice as to the relative location of the restaurant.

"It irritated Alex," Fieldhouse says. "He was an impatient person. If he wanted to go somewhere, he wanted to go. He was not a good guy to be in a car with. On the other hand, he was a wonderful person to be with when he was relaxed."

Given that at times Jordan lacked patience, one would not expect fishing to have been his favorite pastime. He tried it once. Many years later, he related the experience to Art Donaldson.

"I went out on the lake with Jennie," Jordan said.

Satirical postcard sent to lifelong friend Jennie from the New York World's Fair. Postcard provided by Jennie Olson.

"I fished and I fished. Nothing was happening. Finally I just took the tackle box and the pole and threw them over the side. That was the end of my fishing."

That night in New York, Fieldhouse and Jordan — accompanied by Edgar Hellum — made it to the restaurant in Greenwich Village. Unfortunately, they drove in circles trying to find a place to park, it was pouring rain, and when they entered the bar of the establishment there was no place to sit.

"Alex decided we should go someplace else," Fieldhouse says. Jordan stalked out the door and into the middle of the street. He stood in the downpour and directed traffic so Homer could get his car out.

They wound up eating at the Playboy Club (Hellum's wealthy friend had a key), and then when they went out to the car it wouldn't start. There was a foot of water on the street. They took a cab back to the hotel.

The next day, Homer was due at the fairgrounds and Alex volunteered to take care of the car. But when the cab dropped him by the Playboy Club, the car was gone. A mechanic from a garage down the street had it up on a hoist and was making an expensive list of things wrong with it.

Jordan rushed into the garage and in a tone more than one House On The Rock employee would no doubt recognize, told the mechanic to cease and desist. Jordan walked calmly to the car, got inside and turned the key. It started.

Fieldhouse remembers Jordan driving into the fairgrounds that day. "He was pretty proud of himself," Homer says.

They had some fun with the car the day before they were to leave New York. The car was equipped with a telephone that for the trip was inoperable. Nevertheless, Jordan had Fieldhouse drive all over the fairgrounds, with Alex in the passenger seat, talking into the phone that didn't work.

Robert Moses, head of the parks department in New York, was in charge of the World's Fair. As they drove along, Jordan, with the phone up to his ear, would call out to the workmen, "Mr. Moses says he would like to see that stand put over there." He'd point out a location. "It's very important."

Lynn Fieldhouse says of Jordan, "There was an impishness about him. He just couldn't resist pulling people's legs at times; most often it was harmless fun."

"He loved fooling people," John Korb says.

Korb remembers being with Jordan in the Streets of Yesterday, the House's popular re-creation of a 19th Century town, when a woman asked if the trees were real (they look remarkably real — in fact, they're moldings).

"Yes, they're real," Jordan said. "Horticulturists come from around the world to gather acorns off them. These trees only grow in the dark. They're called sabbatical oaks because scientists come here to study them on sabbaticals."

That kind of outlandish claim seems harmless enough, as does another Korb recalls when someone entering the Streets of Yesterday took note of the dim light and asked, "Are we outside?"

"Indeed we are," Jordan said. "We're having a total solar eclipse."

That impish streak would result in a minor brush with the consumer protection authorities in the late 1970s over advertising standards, ending with the House's agreement not to embellish its descriptions of exhibits.

The World's Fair of 1964 may have inspired Jordan, for when he returned to Wisconsin in late March he gave one of his rare interviews — to the Wisconsin State Journal — and even allowed them to take a picture. The photo shows Jordan crouching next to a Japanese-styled yard light of his design.

That '64 State Journal story seems to mark Jordan's first public hint that the House On The Rock might one day expand in dimensions much greater than, say, the Gate House built in 1961.

The State Journal story begins, "Alex Jordan's ultimate effort will put his House On The Rock into the shade . . . The future project will be built on a hillside east of the house. Jordan does not say what it is. Someday work will begin, without a plan on paper. Quite possibly it will join Disneyland, San Simeon and Shangri-la as a super attraction."

Could it be that way back in 1964, Alex Jordan's head was filled with visions of music machines, dollhouses, carousels and cannons?

As the State Journal pointed out, even back then the House's growth was rapid. Nearly 100,000 people toured the House in 1963 (at $1.50 a head) and they would have new construction and art works to view in 1964.

Some of the art would be the product of local artists exhibiting their wares, a practice begun at the House On The Rock in 1963 (when seven artists gave one man shows) and expanded over the years.

A 1968 Capital Times story noted that "area artists will exhibit their works at the House On The Rock weekends during the summer." Nine exhibited over the Fourth of July weekend alone — everything from water color paintings to woodworking and custom costume jewelry.

By 1984, the Madison Area Guide would write, "(Alex Jordan) has peopled 18 new shops with warm-blooded, entirely alive and terrifically talented artists."

In 1964, after his return from New York and the World's Fair, the heart condition that 20 years earlier had kept Jordan out of the army came back to haunt him. He suffered what one of his later doctors referred to as "a massive myocardial infarction" — a severe heart attack.

Jordan survived, but he was hospitalized for a couple of weeks. According to Sid Boyum, it was while hospitalized in 1964 that Jordan was approached by a young man claiming to be his son by a Milwaukee woman. Jordan refused to see him and denied with some vehemence for the rest of his life that he had ever fathered a son.

After Jordan's death in 1989, DNA medical tests were taken, and attorney John Mitby told a probate court judge the tests showed Jordan could not have been the man's father.

"The results of those DNA tests, which I have in writing, exclude the fact that he had this son," Mitby said. "At this point in time, although this person may well believe that he had some relationship with Alex Jordan, the scientific evidence does not support a claim in that belief."

The '64 heart attack did change Jordan's life, at least for a time. He had always lived hard, taking life on his terms — smoking and drinking when he cared to, sleeping irregularly and eating whatever was around when he was hungry. Now, suddenly aware of his own mortality, he slowed down.

The next year, 1965, a writer from the Chicago

75

Tribune observed, "A recent illness prevents him from hefting dirt and stone. He has changed from his work clothes to rumpled corduroy suits. He spends more time in his Gate House office, drafting plans for a new project."

"To relax, he likes to cut and grind telescopic lenses and collect art," the Tribune continued. "His purchases . . . include etchings by Durer, Goya, Holbein, Degas and Cezanne."

Sculptor Tom Kupsh thinks Jordan had a somewhat ambivalent attitude toward modern art. He would denigrate Picasso, then let slip that he'd just bought a Picasso print. He dismissed Jackson Pollock out of hand, mispronouncing his name, perhaps on purpose.

Yet, Jordan and Kupsh discussed Dante's Inferno, and they'd quote poetry back and forth to one another.

"He'd quote the first five lines of 'The Rime of the Ancient Mariner'," Kupsh says, "and I'd give the next five." They both had gone to Catholic boarding schools in northern Wisconsin, where once they teach you Samuel Taylor Coleridge, you remember it.

John Korb remembers Jordan once asking, more or less out of the blue, "Was it the right or left arm extended above in Michaelangelo's statue of the slave?"

If nothing else, he knew art through books. Korb says Alex found the answer to the Michaelangelo question in one of the hundreds — perhaps thousands — of reference works he owned. And not just art books, of course. He had a clearing house in New York — Publisher's Central Bureau Publisher's Close-outs, it was called — with whom he did a brisk business.

His interests were truly eclectic. One day in April of 1970, Gladys Walsh ordered these books for Jordan from the clearing house: Pictorial Album of Aircraft; An Illustrated History of Firearms; 100 Years of Fire-fighting; and Floyd Clymer's Historical Motor Scrapbook of Steam Cars.

A month later, there was another order: The Ancient Art of Warfare; The World Crisis, a six-volume set by Winston Churchill; This Was Sawmilling; A History of the Combat Vessel; and Designing for the Theatre.

Although the '64 heart attack did curtail some of his physical activity (and he did begin taking heart

The Moon Gate is a masonary marvel. Photograph by G.B. Telfair.

medication, including on rare occasions sublingual Nitroglycerin, which Sid Boyum said Alex called his "dynamite pills"), a medical report in 1972 would refer to Jordan's attack eight years earlier and note, "(he) has subsequently made a remarkable recovery."

While Jordan was in the hospital, however, Don Martin, his veteran workman, felt some pressure. Before the attack, Martin says, "Alex was out (at the House) every day. Seven days a week. That made it nice for me. I never had to worry if I was on the right track. Sometimes he'd stay for 10 minutes, sometimes for three hours. He'd basically want to know how things were going."

When Alex was laid up, the next scheduled project was a "Moon Gate", a layered, circular — five foot in diameter — door opening leading to the terraces of the House.

"It was Alex's idea but the plans never got drawn up," Martin says. Consequently, Martin was on his own, and he says it was one of his hardest tasks in more than 30 years of building at the House. He did an excellent job — the stone is beautifully layered.

When Alex got out of the hospital, did he like it? "Well," Martin says, "he didn't tear it down."

Jordan must also have been cheered by the increasing publicity the House was receiving in the press. In 1965, the year after his heart attack, both the <u>Chicago</u> <u>Tribune</u> and the <u>St.</u> <u>Paul</u> <u>Post-Dispatch</u> did major Sunday pieces, complete with color photos.

A respected Wisconsin architect, John W. Steinmann from Monticello, wrote Jordan a letter.

"You're to be commended, Alex," Steinmann wrote, "for a tremendous piece of work. The House On The Rock is probably one of the most interesting architectural achievements I have been privileged to visit. It could only have been accomplished by one who is most sensitive and understanding of the wonders of nature. I am proud to be a friend to the House On The Rock. Each time I come, there are new things to discover, and I look forward to my next visit."

The next truly major project, after the '61 Gate House, was the Mill House, which was three years in construction prior to opening in 1968.

Don Martin worked on it, and recalls, "It has one of the world's largest fireplaces, and all the wood is hand-carved three by five inch pieces that are sanded and stained." It was an ambitious project, and Martin feels Jordan had other plans for the Mill House from the outset.

"I think," Martin says, "that Alex had it in the back of his mind — though he never told me — that he was building a fun entrance to the Streets of Yesterday even then."

The Mill House would indeed serve as an entry into the Streets of Yesterday, but that was still to come when the Mill House opened in 1968.

John Korb feels that when first lady Jackie Kennedy embraced antiquity in refurbishing the White House

G.B. Telfair's wife, Frances, watches Lucifer graze on the roof of the Mill House. Photo by G.B. Telfair.

during the 1960s, it set Jordan to thinking.

"I think Alex, who always had his finger on the pulse of the populace, could see it catching on and began the Mill House," Korb says.

The Mill House opened in 1968. Alex had been very careful in designing this addition so it would not be viewed as just another museum. He felt that men in general did not appreciate wading through museums while on vacation. The Mill House was his attempt at providing something of interest for both genders to enjoy.

The Mill House features a water wheel 14 feet in diameter with a Biblical tableau at its hub, and, of

Lena Jordan
1889 - 1969

Photos provided by
Jennie Olson

course, the mammoth fireplace, with huge cauldrons and a flue so large it contains a stairway leading to a smoke house. The fireplace is patterned after one in a Scottish castle, right down to a secret room deep within the walls, where political refugees could find a temporary haven.

As a 1980 Commerical West magazine piece noted, the Mill House is evidence of Jordan beginning to collect in earnest. "For anyone interested in collecting," the article said, "the tour has really just begun (at the Mill House). Alex Jordan has carried the zeal of the collector to its furthest extreme."

The Mill House opened in 1968. Alex had been very careful in designing this addition so it would not be viewed as just another museum. He felt that men in general did not appreciate wading through museums, while on vacation. The Mill House was his attempt at providing something of interest for both genders to enjoy.

At the entrance of the Mill House is a large bellows that has been converted into a table. Beautiful glass paperweights are displayed in this unique table. Also on display are taxidermy exhibits, mechanical banks, a superb gun collection, and even bisque dolls. There's even exhibits in the rest room at the House On The Rock. Old model railroad engines are featured in the men's room, while interesting glassware from Mexico can be found in the ladies' room.

One of the more interesting, animated music machines, the Hupfeld Violin machine, also makes its home in the Mill House. Three violins and a piano are pneumatically controlled to add more music to this part of the tour.

At the time the Mill House opened to the public, Alex's mother was 80 years old and her health was failing. If Lena had led a full life, she had also endured some tough times.

John Korb's mother used to play cards with Lena, and would return home with stories of how the Jordan residence was overflowing with dolls or copper kettles or whatever Alex was working on at the moment.

In the end, though, she must have been proud of his success, which in fact was just beginning, for when she died on April 4, 1969, she bequeathed some money to the church, but left the bulk of her estate, including her shares in the House On The Rock, to Alex.

It is said the death of the last of one's parents is one of life's great turning points. Alex Jordan, who now owned all the stock in the House, was about to embark in a dramatic new direction.

6   Back to the Future

Many years later, Don Martin would recall the origin of the Streets of Yesterday, "I think Alex may have known in the back of his mind what he wanted, but he went down to Milwaukee to check some things out. He wanted me to go along but he wound up going himself."

He had, in fact, been "going down to Milwaukee" for close to a decade. For it was at the Milwaukee Public Museum that Jordan formed one of the best and most rewarding friendships of his life.

Paul Yank, who today is a sculptor living in Cedarburg, Wisconsin, worked as a sculptor at the Milwaukee Public Museum for 11 years, beginning in 1958. He met Jordan early in his years at the museum, and today recalls his friend with great warmth and affection.

"Alex could have been an architect. He could have been a top contractor. He could have been a sculptor," Yank says. "He could have been any of those things, but he never had time to do that. In a sense, though, he put all those disciplines together in the House.

"He had a lot of latitude there," Yank continues, "and he always had the fortitude to get it done. I admired that in Alex, it was one of the things that drew me to him. He was a very outgoing guy, if he respected you, and also a very hardworking individual. He really wanted to do all these things, and he did them. He pushed the imagination to the limit."

York describes their association as a creative give

and take, and as he speaks, Jordan emerges as both an intensely curious man, and a quick study.

"He found out how to do things right," Yank says. "Everything he wanted to do, that crossed into the museum field, he'd come in and we'd talk about it."

Often the two would go out for lunch or dinner. "I learned a lot of things from him, too," Yank says. "There was always something I could learn from something he did. We'd talk things over. It was never a one-way street. Alex wasn't just a taker. He'd go off with knowledge and I'd go off with knowledge. It was a great friendship."

The friendship began around 1960. Yank was then doing his sculpting in a sort of crow's nest studio on top of a building directly adjacent to the Milwaukee Public Museum. Though technically not closed to the public, it wasn't a place that attracted a lot of visitors.

One day Yank was working on a figure for a diorama — a three-dimensional scene with painted modeled figures and background — when he began feeling like he was being watched. He turned around to see a large man, casually dressed in desert boots, corduroy pants and a shaggy jacket.

"I thought he resembled Yogi Bear," Yank recalls with a laugh. "Alex, of course, was very unpretentious. Somebody probably would have asked if they could help him before he got to me, but nobody wanted to take any time with him. He walked through the building and nobody had any idea who he was or anything else. Finally he got up to my spot which was about the last place you could get before jumping off the building."

Knowing Jordan, this was exactly where he wanted to be. If he was going to learn something, it would be from talking to the creative artist, not a guide or a bureaucrat.

Yank recalls, "He was watching and he was very interested. He just watched and didn't say much. I finally said hello, and he asked about the figure I was working on. I told him about it, and where it was going to go."

The Milwaukee Public Museum was famous around the world for their dioramas. Finally, Jordan introduced himself, and mentioned he had a place near Spring Green, west of Madison, though he wasn't specific about it. And then he asked about the dioramas.

"That's what started us talking," Yank says. "He was

interested in how the rock formations were made. After we had talked for a while, I took him down in back of the diorama and you could see how they were constructed. Then I took him down in the basement where we had some latex rubber molds of the rock formations."

Yank suddenly realized he had spent most of the morning talking with his visitor, and then Jordan said, "Hey, let me take you out to lunch. I know I've taken a lot of your time."

Thus began what would become a tradition with the two men over the years.

"We'd go over to Mader's," Yank says, referring to the famed German restaurant in Milwaukee. "Alex liked weinerschnitzel. He'd always have it. I'd have whatever I wanted and he always picked up the tab."

Though food was never a passion with Jordan to equal some of his other enthusiasms he did enjoy restaurants. In Madison, he and Jennie ate out a fair amount, favoring the Hoffman House East, Poole's Northgate (later Feldman's), and the Chalet St. Moritz on a hill overlooking Middleton.

"He was treated extremely well at Mader's," Yank notes. "Always got a table, no problem."

That first day, the two men had really hit it off well. They saw each other quite a bit in the 1960s, as Jordan began to expand the House On The Rock. At that time, Alex was particularly concerned with keeping the natural look of the original House, even though some of the things he wanted to do meant an exposed beam here and there.

Yank showed him some museum tricks for the dioramas. They made latex molds off natural rock, and could then reproduce pieces that looked like actual stone and could be used to cover a beam. "A geologist might be able to tell the difference, but the average person could never tell," Yank says.

Yank adds that Jordan was a fast learner. "He was a master working with materials." As the House kept growing, there was more to learn. "As the House was developing," Yank says, "he'd want to know how some of the different things we were doing were made. We got into doing fiberglass with some of our figures, to make them lighter, so they'd be put more easily in motion. I showed him how we were doing it."

In the late '60s, one Milwaukee Public Museum exhibit in particular captured Jordan's interest. It was an authentic-looking re-creation of old-time Milwaukee called the "Streets of Old Milwaukee."

Yank was working with huge latex molds to make the trees for the exhibit. In fact, Yank at the time authored an article for National Museum Magazine suggesting they were likely the largest latex molds ever made.

"Alex came by while I was working on them," Yank says, "and I think he learned a lot from it. He learned from our mistakes, so in fact he was ahead of us when he did the Streets of Yesterday."

It was the success of the Mill House that convinced Jordan to attempt a more ambitious display of antiquity. The Mill House, of course, had antique guns, dolls, and suits of armour.

"The reception was so warm," Korb says, "and the response so enthusiastic, Alex said, 'Hey, I've hit on something. Let's do something more,' and he began construction on the Streets of Yesterday."

The Streets are Don Martin's favorite exhibit in the House, and why not? His fingerprints are all over it. The area where Grandma's House now stands was his original workshop, but as it grew, he says, "my workshop just kept backing up."

Of the Streets, Martin says, "That I enjoyed. You see, by that time I was getting to be more of a carpenter." They worked on it one building at a time. "We just went up one side of the street and down the other," Martin says.

Working directly under Martin during the construction of the Streets was Bob Searles, who had worked at the Villa Louis Museum in Prairie du Chien, Wisconsin. Jordan hired him in 1970, and since working at the House On The Rock was always something Searles had dreamed about, he didn't have to give it much thought. Searles worked at the House On The Rock for approximately three years. Working closely with Jordan, Searles further developed the skills that later would make him a successful porcelain sculptor.

The Streets of Yesterday opened to the public in 1971. Of the exhibit, Paul Yank, of the Milwaukee Museum, says, "It's authentic. The craftsmanship is wonderful. Some of Alex's re-creations are superior to those at good museums."

The Streets of Yesterday under construction. Photo by G.B. Telfair.

According to Yank, Jordan was a stickler for historical accuracy. An old-time sheriff's office, for instance, would have specific particulars about it. It would have a certain look.

"He'd get pictures," Yank says. "He'd get all the information he could. It's what I did at the Museum. I told him you had to be a historian also. You research and you research and when you've got all you can, you do it."

Yank says Jordan was good enough that knowledgeable people would tour the Streets and think a Jordan re-creation was 19th century artifact. "Alex really tried to get it right," he says. "I know of Museum people who went through and were amazed at the things he could get. Well, those were his own creations."

A view down the Streets of Yesterday. Photo from the House On The Rock archives.

Open now for two decades, the Streets of Yesterday remains a favorite of many. The Uplands, a guide to Southwestern Wisconsin, observed that the Streets "introduces you to the charming nostalgia of the 1880s. You'll be able to see horses, shops, and stores reminiscent of this period. The lighting even simulates an old-fashioned, gas-illuminated bricked street.

"As usual, Jordan has paid particular attention to each and every detail; from the sleeping Dalmation at the fire station to all the remedies of the oldest farmer's almanac and the newest sure-cures require on display at the apothecary's shop. There's grandma's house, a toy store, a barber shop, a sheriff's office, a corsetier's shop, and many other quaint, little shops that take you back in time.

"The entire street resounds with the melodies coming from the cymbals, calliope pipes, bells, bottles, jugs and drums which comprise the Great Calliope found at the end of the street — the first of Jordan's magnificent music machines to go on display."

Funny touches abound. At the Apothecary, a sign advertises live tapeworms to help lose weight. At the sheriff's office, a three-fingered hand is preserved in a jar of formaldehyde.

The Gladiator Calliope, at the end of the street, with its Sousa and Dixieland tunes, evokes New Orleans.

"People loved it," Korb says. "Alex thought, 'Why not give them a whole street of music?' "

So work began on the Music of Yesterday, which, when it opened three years later, would feature perhaps the greatest collection in the world of animated, automated music machines and gigantic pipe organs.

Alex Jordan, however, almost didn't live to see it. In 1972 Jordan was 58 years old, and still making the daily commute from Madison out to the House On The Rock.

The town of Arena is located on Highway 14, ten miles east of Spring Green. On the evening of December 6, 1972, Jordan was alone in his car — a 1972 Ford station wagon — when just outside of Arena he collided with a horse.

"That damn horse's timing couldn't have been better if we planned the thing together," Jordan told a Milwaukee Journal reporter three years later. "The car was totaled and so was I, just about. I fractured my skull, jaw and leg in that one. Oh, yeah, and my neck, too. I was a quadrepeligic for a while."

According to a medical report, after the initial collision, "the horse then bounced up and landed on the top of the car."

An Iowa County ambulance transported Jordan to Methodist Hospital in Madison. He was in rough shape. Gladys Walsh, whom Jordan had asked the sheriff to call from the accident scene, later observed that Alex had suffered lacerations to his nose and the top of his head, a broken neck, shattered vertebrae, and partial paralysis of his right arm and leg, as well as his left arm.

In the House corporate minutes, Walsh noted Jordan was "in great pain, in traction, and at times irrational."

On December 15, 1972, Jordan underwent a four and one half hour operation in which bone was grafted from elsewhere in his body to his neck. The procedure was called an anterior spinal fusion.

He remained hospitalized for 70 days. After his release in mid-February of 1973, he returned to the hospital five days a week on an outpatient basis. He would continue as an outpatient throughout 1973. It was a very serious accident.

"He broke his neck in three places," John Korb recalls. "The doctors not only said he wouldn't walk. They said he wouldn't live."

When he heard about the accident, Paul Yank drove to Madison from Milwaukee to see his friend.

"My God," Yank recalls, "he looked like he would never be a working individual again. He was all broken up. He was walking sideways."

But Yank remembered the first time he saw Jordan after the accident, Alex stated his determination to come all the way back.

"He was bound and determined he was going to recover," Yank says. "The average person would have died. Alex still had things he wanted to do in life, and he was going to do them."

Jordan paid $5,000 for a 1973 Ford station wagon (he favored station wagons, and later vans, because he could load them in back with materials for the House), although it was almost a year before he could drive himself. Lynn Fieldhouse's father drove him back and forth to the House. One day many months later, in typical Jordan fashion, Alex turned to him and said simply, "I can drive myself today."

On December 21, 1973 — a year and two weeks after his accident — Jordan saw his doctor. The doctor noted, "patient states that he is slowly improving. He says a couple of months ago he was unable to fire an antique pistol with the right hand but now he can . . . He states that he has some sensory changes of both arms and the left leg. He has less pain about the shoulders. Seldom has pain about the neck." He was on the road to a remarkable recovery.

If the early '70s had some low moments for Jordan, good things happened to him as well. Work at the House on the Music of Yesterday was progressing. In those years Jordan would also make three associations with individuals who played important roles in the last two decades of his life.

They were John Korb, whom he had known since the '40s but who would become the House's first real general manager in the early '70s; John Mitby, who would become his attorney; and Art Donaldson, the Janesville businessman who would eventually purchase the House On The Rock.

As a young boy, John Korb had had an unusual introduction to Alex Jordan. It was the late '40s and Korb and his brother had been invited to the Jordan home by Alex's mother, Lena, to see for the first time a new invention called television. The Jordans, at the time, were living at 104 Langdon Street, the corner of Langdon and Carroll Streets.

They were just starting to watch the television, with its grainy picture, when a tall brawny man in his middle 30s burst into the house, tossed his leather jacket on the couch, yelled, "Ma, I need something to eat" and bustled into the kitchen. It was Alex, back from a day of hauling stone and mortar at Deer Shelter Rock.

"Don't worry, boys," Lena Jordan said, "he won't hurt you."

It was not an inappropriate way to meet the often fiery Jordan. Korb came to know him well in the '50s and '60s, and served as a pallbearer at the funerals of both of Alex's parents.

By 1974 Korb was working in real estate and apartment management for his brother and his wife, who owned 51 buildings in the Madison area.

One evening in August of 1974, Korb was checking on a building when Jordan pulled up in his station wagon and waved him over.

"I want you to come out and work at the House On The Rock," Jordan said.

"In what capacity?" Korb asked, reasonably enough.

Jordan rattled off a string of four-letter words. "Alex was quite adept at profanity," Korb says, adding he seldom employed it in mixed company. "It never really meant anything."

Jordan shouted, "I need a manager! What do you think! Come by my place tonight and we'll discuss it!" Korb showed up at 8:00 p.m.

"Well, you know, Korb," Jordan began, "I have a

bed to sleep in. I've got a refrigerator to keep my food from spoiling. I've got some money — I don't know exactly how much — but I've got every damn thing I need except one."

"What's that?" Korb asked.

"I don't have anyone to say, 'Alex, you're an ass.' "

It was Jordan's way of saying he needed some informed dissent on occasion.

"He knew he intimidated people," Korb says. "That night he said, 'Everyone at the House On The Rock is terrified of me. If I look at a waterfall and say, "Should I put a green or blue light on it," they're not going to give their opinion on which looks better. They're going to tell me what they think I want to hear.' "

It's doubtful Korb — or anyone else at the House — ever reached the point where they could comfortably call Jordan "an ass," and even disagreeing was sometimes risky. As Don Martin said of the Streets of Yesterday, "I have a few ideas in there, but let's face it — Alex liked to have his way in the end."

Korb did sign on as general manager, a post he would hold until 1988. He was 32 at the time he took the job — well-traveled, outgoing and good with people. He became, in a sense, Jordan's link to the public, or at least to the press.

When disappointed reporters found they couldn't actually speak with the creator of this wonder they had just toured, Korb smoothed their feathers and spun out a few good anecdotes to make them happy.

It couldn't always have been easy. Korb once told a reporter Jordan was "married" to the House, and Alex exploded. What right did Korb have to say that? (It seems reasonable enough — few marriages have bonds as strong as those between Alex Jordan and the House On The Rock.)

Korb was walking a tightrope, and for a long time he did it well. He allowed his brilliant, mercurial boss what he needed and treasured most — privacy.

As the House grew and the money rolled in, Jordan was not only forced to guard his privacy, he felt, at least on some level, a sense of the whole thing getting away from him, of his control slipping.

It was late in 1974, shortly after hiring Korb, that on a Saturday morning Jordan made a phone call to a young Madison attorney named John Mitby.

Mitby had graduated from law school in 1971, worked in Green Bay for a couple of years, and in 1973 came back to Madison to join the Axley Brynelson Law Firm. He had handled some entertainment-type clients, including helping former UW basketball coach John Powless get started in the indoor tennis business.

Mitby had been recommended to Jordan by an accounting firm both had worked with. Still, he was surprised and flattered to get the call.

"I was a young lawyer," Mitby says. "How many people would have come to me? I had never seen a million dollar deal before."

Mitby recalls his first impression of Jordan: "I think to a certain extent, the public was starting to overwhelm him. He was a private man and people were calling him at home. For a long time he had a listed number. People would call and ask where they could buy something.

"By the time he called me," Mitby continues, "Alex had created one of the largest attractions in Wisconsin. He had become inundated. And as the publicity increased, it suddenly became an economic reality. Because of that, it started to attract people who were interested in buying it or at least finding out if it was for sale."

That was the purpose of the Saturday call late in 1974. Somebody was interested in the House On The Rock, a tentative offer had been made. Could Mitby look it over?

They met at Mitby's office. Jordan explained that he didn't really want to sell the House, because over the years his practice had been to put most of the profits back into it. Alex wasn't sure a new owner would continue this practice.

"He had always wanted to give people a taste of something special," Mitby says, "and if they appreciated that, then he'd give them a larger taste. That was part of his philosophy as the House grew. Every year there would be something different or more spectacular than last year."

That attitude, coupled with Jordan's unceasing extravagance where the House was concerned — "if a project required ten dolls," Mitby says, "it ended up being 100 dolls" — had led Jordan to reluctantly entertain thoughts of selling.

Mitby recalls, "He had thought that possibly for the

House On The Rock to be able to continue to expand, he might need to sell all or part of it or perhaps take on a partner."

The first meeting took only 45 minutes. Mitby looked over the documents — "the House was worth between one and three million at the time," the attorney says — and wasn't impressed. Among other problems with the offer was a lack of money up front, coupled with some questions about the buyer's credit worthiness.

"Alex," Mitby says, "I don't think this is in your best interest." Mitby was a little nervous making that pronouncement. But Jordan simply asked four or five questions, direct and to the point, and then said, "I agree with you." Mitby's experience echoed that of others over the years. Once Jordan made a decision about you, if it was positive and he trusted you, he seldom looked back.

Nevertheless, there was the fact that the House was expanding, coupled with Jordan's relative lack of liquidity.

"I'm not sure how you solve it," Mitby said.

"I have a solution," Jordan said. "But it's something I don't want to do."

"What's that?" the attorney asked.

"Raise my ticket prices."

Which he did. Mitby would recall that several years later, Jordan called him with a different problem — but resolved it with a similar solution.

"I have too many people going through this place," Jordan said, and thus causing wear and tear. "I'm going to have to raise my ticket prices again to get the number of people down."

Mitby would remain Jordan's lawyer until the latter's death, and would also handle Jordan's estate. Alex had another trusted attorney, Frank Hamilton of Dodgeville, who handled most of his real estate transactions.

Mitby was involved with potiential buyers — and there were several over the years — as well as with a variety of governmental agencies, some of which didn't know quite what to make of the House On The Rock.

"It was not your average business," Mitby says. There were a few encounters with officials from the Wisconsin Department of Revenue. Mitby recalls, "There was an ongoing battle about whether the things he bought were appreciating or depreciating. They just didn't understand it."

Like many creative people, Jordan despised paperwork with much relish, which didn't make dealing with bureaucracies any easier. Mitby, though, says Gladys Walsh "took care of the paperwork" and was very conscientious about it.

"Even when she had become quite old," Mitby says, "she used to come up to my office on crutches and say, 'Alex wanted you to take a look at this.' "

Mitby disputes any notion that Jordan might not have minded making an end run around the revenue bureaucrats.

"I represented him since 1974," Mitby says. "I never saw any evidence of not paying taxes, of having anything offshore or strange, or problems of not paying bills. If someone tried to overcharge him, well, yeah, he'd question it. He didn't appreciate getting taken.

"He kept every ticket going back years," Mitby continues. "Boxes and boxes of every ticket sold at the House. If a tax guy wanted to count tickets, he could count tickets."

Jordan's insatiable thirst for collecting, and his lack of enthusiasm for writing much down, also made things interesting when a potential buyer came along. While Mitby feels Jordan was never truly interested in selling until the last few years of his life, he didn't mind entertaining offers, for "If they were that interested it showed he was doing something right."

One of Jordan's most intriguing suitors, in the late 1970s, was the Wisconsin Alumni Research Foundation (WARF), a University of Wisconsin connected enterprise that had deep pockets as well as some properties already in the Wisconsin Dells.

"Actually, that got somewhat close to a deal," Mitby says. "Alex was very interested. He thought WARF was large enough to really make (the House) take off."

Always, Mitby recalls, Jordan "was very concerned about what his role would be in the House if he should sell."

With hindsight, you can guess the WARF deal had little chance to go through from the outset. Jordan had little use for bureaucracies, committees — any kind of group-think — and for all their assets and influence, WARF was a very large organization.

At the time of the WARF discussions, the House was worth in the neighborhood of $5-$7 million. The proposed deal called for Jordan to transfer his assets to them and he would receive a lifetime annuity.

But WARF had a couple of problems. First, they weren't sure they had anyone who could service all the House's exhibits — the computerized music machines of the Music of Yesterday were in place by that time, as well as other complicated (not to mention unique) machinery.

More immediately, they were having trouble evaluating assets. Finally WARF sent an accountant out to meet with Jordan and Mitby at the House. He studied the asset sheet and settled on the baby grand pianos. Jordan had listed five baby grands as assets.

"Let's go see them," the WARF representative said. They were, if nothing else, easy to count. After touring the House they found only three.

Mitby turned to Jordan and said, "Are there other baby grands?"

Jordan shrugged. "Sure, but they're over in the shop."

The three men walked over to the workshop area where they did not find two additional baby grand pianos. They found <u>29</u> — for a total of 32 baby grands. The WARF man was shaking his head. Mitby said, "Alex, what gives?"

Jordan replied, "Well, they aren't in the House yet, so I don't really count them."

Mitby can laugh about it now. "He had accumulated and acquired things and he had it all in his mind." After Jordan's death, Mitby was going through things at the House and found the first-ever Sears catalogue in a box of stuff. "Once he saw something, he remembered it," Mitby says, "but it could drive us nuts."

The man who eventually did buy the House On The Rock was not thinking of purchasing it when he first met Alex Jordan in the 1970s. Indeed, it took a lot of effort on his part just to <u>meet</u> Jordan. But then, working hard had never been a problem for Art Donaldson.

As a boy growing up in Janesville, Wisconsin, Donaldson had mowed lawns and put up lemonade stands and sold greeting cards. It wasn't money for money's sake, but rather, as he said many years later in an interview, "You can't create things, build things, do things, unless you have money."

After finishing high school and a tour of duty in the Army, Donaldson resettled in Janesville and went to work. He began a small billboard and sign company and before long was successful enough that he was buying out some competitors.

Donaldson's style in business is personal and hands-on; like Jordan, he's an unpretentious man more comfortable in a work shirt and pants than a pin-striped suit.

Years later, after Donaldson had built his company into a seven-figure operation, the president of Tommy Bartlett, Inc. in the Dells — a Donaldson client — told the Milwaukee Journal, "He still calls on companies when, normally, you'd expect somebody who has made a million several times over to let other people do the work."

That was still in the future, of course, the first time Donaldson called on the House On The Rock in the middle '70s. His sign and billboard business had sparked his interest in tourism and attractions, however, and he looked forward, not only of trying to sell the House some signs, but also meeting the man behind it, Alex Jordan.

Easier said than done. It took Donaldson nearly a year to meet Jordan the first time. Each time Donaldson stopped, he was intercepted by John Korb, then general manager, who was friendly, but adamant.

"Do you have an appointment to see Mr. Jordan?"

"No," Donaldson said.

"Mr. Jordan won't see you," Korb said.

This happened a couple more times until in exasperation Donaldson finally said, "How am I ever going to meet this guy?"

He wasn't expecting Korb's reply. "Call him up at home at one or two in the morning and see if you can't get an appointment."

Well, Donaldson didn't want to do that. What he didn't know is that Jordan had kept iconoclastic hours most of his adult life. A daily log he kept in the 1980s for a heart monitor shows that he actually slept twice during any 24 hour period, usually from around 6 p.m. to 10 p.m., and then again from 5 a.m. to 8 a.m. (Most of the remaining nightime hours were spent reading; the daytime hours supervising at the House On The Rock.)

Not knowing that, Donaldson was reluctant to call. He tried stopping at the House one more time. "Call him in the middle of the night!" Korb said.

Finally, with nothing really to lose, Donaldson called Jordan at 2 a.m. Alex answered and the two men talked for nearly an hour. And as Donaldson recalls, "He agreed to give me an appointment."

Not only that, Donaldson's first appointment, a few days later, was successful.

"After I talked to him," Donaldson says, "I found out one of his real loves was signs. He didn't talk to hardly any sales people, but he'd talk to somebody who had some signs. I think I sold him some signs that first day."

The two began to form a friendship, and among other things, Jordan impressed Donaldson with his business acumen.

"As the years went by, I developed about as good a friendship as you could develop with Alex," Donaldson says. "He didn't allow many intrusions into his life."

Donaldson enjoyed stopping at the House On The Rock. "It was an interesting call to make," he says, "if he was in the mood to talk. He had a broad knowledge of the business world. I've met a lot of people, and I think he had the best overall grasp of the total goings-on of business of anyone I've ever met. I could talk to him on commodities, metals, and interest rates. He understood them all."

But as Donaldson says, Jordan's application of that knowledge was on a narrow track.

"He did very little to apply it," Donaldson notes. "He focused on the House On The Rock. Everything came back to it."

Asked years later when he first thought he might like to own the House, Donaldson says, "I think from the first time I saw it. But I never thought it would even be possible."

His appreciation of the House was immediate and profound. "It's entertaining, it's alive, it's not like a museum," Donaldson says. "It does something to everyone who goes there. It gets to their soul in some form or fashion."

Donaldson's later travels would render him even more impressed. "I've traveled the world over several times. To me the House On The Rock is a Rembrandt of the world. It's a creation that can never be duplicated, from the genius standpoint, to the cost standpoint. The cost of duplication would be astronomical today. Nor could you find a lot of those things."

Sometime after they met, Jordan turned to Donaldson one day and said, "You know, I'd sell this place."

Donaldson, unsure of how serious Alex was, replied, "Well, I'd sure like to figure out how I could buy it."

By that time, Donaldson knew Jordan was a great one to give a short answer.

"Hmmmmmm," Alex said.

The time would come eventually when he'd be serious. For now, his mind was alive with plans and ideas. In a sense, even as he approached 60, Jordan had just begun.

7   The Great Collector

Alex Jordan was always — <u>always</u> — on the lookout for things. Often there didn't seem to be a plan, or even a rhyme or reason. If something was unique, interesting or unusual, there was a good chance he wanted it. If he liked it enough, he wanted many others like it as well. So often in his life, Alex Jordan wanted it <u>all</u>.

"I always said that Alex's hobby was collecting other people's hobbies," Korb said. "Dolls, circus miniatures, guns, organs, you-name-it. He did almost all of it over the telephone."

"He'd place a bid or send a finder out to evaluate a collection," Korb said. "If the finder liked it, he would say so when he called back. They'd discuss it, and then Alex would sanction the purchase."

Don Martin concurs, "He bought a lot of stuff over the phone — through pictures — without ever going out to look at them."

Jordan's well-known distaste for travel, or at least being away from the House On The Rock, may have had something to do with that. But sculptor Paul Yank, formerly of the Milwaukee Public Museum, says Jordan's collecting was anything but haphazard.

"I'd take him into the gun collection at the Museum," Yank says. "We had some great guns in there. He could see what was really hard to get — what was rare. He was doing research. When he went to gun auctions he knew what was special and what wasn't."

Yank says he was always impressed with both the scope of Jordan's vision and his ambition.

"Any kind of collection he wanted to know about," Yank says, "he'd come down and I'd take him over and we'd look at them. He sure developed into a collector. Look at the organs! He started collecting them from all the theatres, buying them up and then bringing them all together. The idea of trying that from scratch is just amazing. I like collecting, and I always figure I'll use something sometime. Most people never do, they forget about them. Alex did it. He put things to use."

According to Yank, Jordan's passion for his organ collection included a strong desire to find and bring them to the House in good shape.

"Getting them out without destroying them was an enormous project," Yank says. "Anybody can take things out but then destroy them in the process. Alex saved them with loving care. It cost him a lot to get it done."

Yank mentioned guns. Jordan's eventual gun collection was much appreciated by someone who should know best, Jerome Rakusan, the editor of Guns magazine. After Rakusan visited the House with his family, he wrote back enthusiastically:

"One of the most unique settings for a gun collection is located in southwestern Wisconsin . . . The gun collection is almost as unique as the building which houses it. It is a collection for those who wish to admire old guns; not especially for those who want to study them.

"This collection is not so much for the serious student of firearms as it is for those who enjoy looking at handsome gun decorations and intricate mechanisms. The advanced collector will find some striking examples of museum quality firearms which reflect not only historical associations, but periods in the development of firearms.

"There are a number of fine firearms in this collection," Rakusan continued, "that will interest those who are students of the rare and significant. It is a fun collection, and one that can be enjoyed by both the serious collector and the layman."

The Guns magazine editor concluded: "One of the nice parts about visiting the House On The Rock with a family is that while you stand in front of the display cases filled with firearms, your wife will probably be just as intent as she studies the collection of antique glassware in the women's lounge or the nostalgic collection of dolls and toys found in the Doll House. Meanwhile, the children will be fascinated with the mechanical banks."

Like the House's gun collection, the Music of Yesterday, opened to the public in 1974, is an amalgamation of genuine artifacts and re-creations designed and built on the House property. John Hovancak, of Dodgeville, Wisconsin, had a great deal to do with creating this exciting addition.

In 1986, the Home News Vacation Guide found the Music of Yesterday to be the "most marvelous" exhibit at the House. The writer was given a tour by House general manager (at the time), John Korb.

"These music machines call up scenes of 19th Century Europe," Home News observed, "where they were once part of popular culture, predating the phonograph. They were most likely to be found in public gathering places — hotel lobbies, saloons and the like.

"Visitors stand before huge cabinets or rooms filled with violins, cellos, woodwinds, drums and bells with air hoses or pneumatic tubes attached to the instruments. You drop in a coin and the music begins."

The Home News writer explained further: "The orchestrions rely partly on illusion. You think you are actually hearing the instruments moving before you, but the strings and woodwinds do not actually play. Their sound is simulated by organ pipes. Some instruments — xylophones, accordians, and bells — actually do play. Some machines have animated figures actually playing the drums."

Korb explained, "The whole thing is pneumatically done. There are relays, there is a paper roll that drives it through a tracker bar which is all controlled by vacuum. Each instrument is played with air on a pneumatic system, exactly like that of a piano player."

A La Crosse man, David Kraehenbuehl, took over the music portion of the exhibits in 1982 and told the La Crosse Tribune, "I had no idea, really, what I was getting into. It's all a kind of crazy, fantastic game."

It's a game that got somewhat easier for him, Kraehenbuehl explained, when the House purchased a

Jordan discreetly dedicated the Gladiator Calliope to his lifelong companion, Jennie Olson. Note the reference to "Jenny's Landing" beneath the "Gladiator" inscripton. Photo by G.B. Telfair.

computer system and reworked the exhibits into the computer. While Kraehenbuehl supplied the music, it was the computer know-how of Pete Ewenko who brought it all together.

From the time of their installation, however, certain pieces of the music machines have stood out and consistently delighted visitors. The <u>Home News</u> described the favorites:

"The Gladiator Calliope (located at the end of the Streets of Yesterday), a huge animated music machine that Alex Jordan designed himself, was built in the House On The Rock's own workshop. The machine looks like a marching band aboard a steamboat. A half dozen wooden soldiers about three feet high move their limbs and heads while they seem to play or conduct. The music actually comes from partly concealed player pianos and organ pipes."

The Mikado, a favorite to many, is another Jordan design. It has an Oriental theme and two haunting musical selections, "Dance Macabre" and the "Ritual Fire Dance". Two life-size Oriental figures, made of papier mache, are highly animated. One plays an elaborate flute and his cheeks actually puff in and out. The other plays a large kettle drum, and as they both play, their bright eyes scan the room, eyebrows raised, and mustaches bob up and down.

It's clear that in the decade since he went to the New York World's Fair to study Disney's animated Lincoln, Alex Jordan had learned a thing or two about animation.

The magnificent Blue Room. Photo from the House On The Rock archives.

Continuing in the Music of Yesterday, the Blue Room — features an orchestrion, a mechanically operated symphony orchestra. This exhibit was fashioned after Queen Victoria's 1867 railroad coach.

Others may prefer the Franz Josef orchestrion. It's in a cabinet 28 feet tall. There's a square grand piano in it, bells, a cello, a triangle, percussion, a sousaphone, clarinets, a xylophone and a bass drum.

Finally, there's the Regina Sublima — an antique dating back to 1893 — a metal disc player enclosed in a wooden cabinet.

While the Regina Sublima is a real antique, as are many other pieces and exhibits at the House, everyone knows that other pieces are re-creations designed and built on the House property. It's part of the fun — guessing what's real at the House and what is the magic of imagination and re-creation.

It is fun — as long as everyone knows that guessing is part of the game. In 1978, the House had a brush with the State Justice Department's Office of Consumer Protection after a disgruntled employee blew the whistle on some misrepresentations.

It's not surprising that an attraction as big as the House — not to mention a personality as powerful as Alex Jordan — produced a disgruntled employee or two.

Greg Burke, general manager, started working at the House On The Rock in 1977. He acknowledges Jordan could be tough to work for, but points out he also gave chances to people with limited experience, some of whom later turned on him.

Burke himself was hired green by the shop foreman at the time. Work was beginning on the Organ Room.

"Do you have any experience in pipe organs?" the foreman asked.

"No," Burke replied.

"Any experience in electronics — or electrical work?"

"No," Burke said again.

"Well," the foreman said, "can you start tomorrow?"

Burke continues, "Tom Kupsh was a sculptor, but a lot of people who lacked training were allowed to come in and paint things like carousel animals. Those folks weren't paid high wages, but they didn't deserve high wages. They learned and got their start here."

Burke also saw his employer abused. "The minute Alex drove off the property," Burke says, "there were people who started sitting around. There were people who drank on the clock, and they got fired for it. And then you have disgruntled employees."

Tom Kupsh says that three weeks into the job, certain individuals came to him and began trying to — in effect — poison the well against Jordan.

"Everyone takes it for granted he did things to people," Kupsh says. "He was a strong and powerful man. But people did things to him as well." Of the wage situation, Kupsh adds, "Some of those people weren't worth very much money."

Certainly the disgruntled employee who went to the consumer protection authorities was within his rights. The House had been representing the Mikado as having been built in Holland in 1914; and the Franz Josef as having been presented to the Austrian Emperor in 1898 to commemorate the 50th anniversary of his reign.

The episode ended quietly with the House agreeing not to embellish in its advertising and promotion. If it wasn't that big a deal, Jordan still regretted it.

"He learned the hard way about those things," Tom Kupsh says. "I think he recognized the criticism was justified. He felt bad when it happened. He worried about it and said Jennie was upset about it too."

It seems clear mischief, as opposed to any dark deception, was at the root of the controversy. John Korb was standing with Jordan next to the Mikado when Jordan was contemplating what year to put on it.

"How about 1914?" Jordan said. "That's a good year. That's the year I was born."

Jordan himself told the Wisconsin State Journal in a 1978 interview that it was just a matter of getting carried away.

"It was a little too much showbiz," he said. "I started it, and others just followed, each adding a little more."

Bruce Craig, the assistant attorney general who handled the investigation, spoke to the State Journal and seemed satisfied the House had learned its lesson.

"It was difficult for us to decide whether Jordan, who has clearly put a lot of time and money into the displays, set out to deliberately lie to the public or whether he was just out to flavor things."

Craig decided it was the latter, and concluded, "I

think what Jordan decided, somewhere down the line, was that what he was doing out there was impressive enough that it wasn't necessary to guild the lily. Show business people are used to puffing things up. Rather than being a crook, he was just someone who got carried away."

Sculptor Tom Kupsh was one of the employees closest to Jordan over the years, as well as one of the most articulate and astute observers of the House's complex creator.

Kupsh began working at the House in August of 1977. He had yet to meet Jordan when he first came to work at 8 a.m. on August 17. Down in the workshop, work was progressing on what would become the world's largest carousel. They were restoring and repairing animals for the carousel.

Educated and trained as a sculptor, Kupsh was in his element. That morning he found some scrap wood, carved a leg for a horse, and attached it.

About noon, Jordan came into the shop. Word had reached Kupsh that Alex wasn't convinced he needed a real sculptor at the House (more likely, he was concerned about having to pay "real sculptor" wages).

Jordan approached Kupsh and said, "What have they got you doing?"

"Just this thing with the horse," Kupsh recalled.

Jordan noticed the new leg. "Where did that come from?"

"I carved it," Kupsh said.

Jordan raised his eyebrows. Then he walked over to the carousel and pointed to a fiberglass lion. He had some changes he wanted Kupsh to make — reshape the head a little and make the teeth larger.

Jordan did have a good eye and a sixth sense about what would work in an exhibit, right up to the end of his life. Art Donaldson notes, "He had such a good eye. Somebody would be setting something up, he'd look at it, and he'd go move three or four things this way or that, and it would look perfect."

He may have been unprepared for Kupsh's method with the fiberglass lion that day in 1977. After giving his instructions, Jordan wandered off. Kupsh took a reciprocating saw and totally demolished the lion, save for the head.

It made quite a noise, and Kupsh looked up to see

Jordan hurrying back, with, the sculptor recalls, "a little bit of alarm in his eyes."

Kupsh thought, "Well, I'm either going to be fired or he's going to give me a chance."

Jordan said, "I suppose you know what you're doing?"

"Yeah," Kupsh said. "No problem."

Jordan nodded and left. When he returned the next day, Kupsh had the lion all back together, the improvements accomplished. Jordan looked at it for a moment, then said, "Well, I guess we've finally got an artist on the staff."

It was to be a mutually rewarding relationship for many years. In his first 15 weeks at the House, Kupsh built 15 animals for the carousel. Jordan would come in and say something like, "I want a kangaroo."

"How big?" Kupsh would ask.

"Oh, you know," Jordan would say. Often they'd peruse books and magazines for ideas.

"Alex and I generated the stuff, and then it went up to the painters," Kupsh said. He credits Mark Miller and Jim McKahn with "starting the painting technique of the House On The Rock." There is, Kupsh says, a certain look that works well with three-dimensional figures. "You work dark to light," he says. "It's a lively technique."

The animals they sent to the painters that first year included a kangaroo, a three-headed dragon, and a series of centaurs — a woman's head and torso on animal legs.

One day in October of 1977 Alex and Jennie drove up in a van. They had a rather ugly fiberglass pig in the back. "Maybe you can make a bulldog out of this," Alex said. Jennie looked skeptical. "If you can, that's pretty good," she said.

They did a good enough job that when the "Ripley's Believe It Or Not" network television show featured the House, the hostess opened the program sitting on the bulldog.

"When Alex came in I always tried to have something for him to look at," Kupsh said. "Always. That's what he wanted. Something to look at."

In appreciation, Jordan made Kupsh one of the best-paid employees at the House, and also began a practice of bringing the sculptor presents including, for a time, a bottle of whiskey every week. Kupsh

The Bulldog, a favorite for many, is shown here during the construction of the world's largest carousel. Photo by G.B. Telfair.

accepted, although he wasn't close to being in that league as a drinker.

"Keep a bottle on the job," Jordan told him with a wink. "For snake bite and inspiration."

They'd talk about everything under the sun except the internal politics of the House On The Rock. It was, Kupsh thinks in retrospect, a way for the mercurial Jordan to relax.

"In eight years he never raised his voice to me," Kupsh said. "He told me when he retired he was going

Don Martin mounting lights on the Carousel. Photo by G.B. Telfair.

to buy an easy chair and — horror of horrors — just sit and watch me work. He didn't get to do it. He was never going to really retire."

As the months turned into years there were lions, tigers and elephants — 18 rows of animals, 269 in all, by the time the carousel opened. Don Martin and his crew, meanwhile, were working on the lights. "One winter," Martin recalls, "we did nothing but mount lights." The carousel would eventually have over 20,000 lights.

One of Kupsh's best projects wasn't for the carousel. One day Jordan came to him and said, "I'm going to make you, not only very rich, but also a very famous man.

It was Alex's way of saying he was excited about a project.

It turned out he wanted Kupsh to sculpt the Four Horsemen of the Apocalypse, which he did. It's an excellent piece of work, and in a nice moment some time after Jordan's death, Kupsh was rummaging around in the shop when he found a plaque with his name on it, crediting him for the Four Horsemen.

Some people felt Kupsh might be gaining too much prominence, and so Jordan asserted himself. In any case, it was percursory to the time in early 1984 when Kupsh felt the need to move on.

He moved to the West Coast, but would later return to work at the House On The Rock in the last months of Jordan's life, and they would mend their fences.

Kupsh was still at the House when the Carousel Building opened in 1981. Two other exhibits had opened in the late 1970s. The Little Streets of Yesterday featured the shops and offices of various artisans and professionals, including a dental clinic, eye clinic, lamp shop, music box shop, and a local farm machinery shop.

The Red Room, opened in 1978. A massive chandelier dominates the room while numerous lights and mirrors further enchance the room. There is also a sleigh being drawn by a tiger and lion.

The best was yet to come. In 1979 <u>Wisconsin State Journal</u> reporter Richard Jaeger caught up with Jordan and Korb one day while they and the crew were hard at work on the Organ Room (it was tentatively called the "Inferno Room" back then). After a time, Jordan took the reporter to an adjacent building, where he flipped a switch.

"How about that?" Jordan said, softly, but proudly. Jaeger wrote his answer in his story, describing "a display that is sure to take the breath away of everyone who views it."

It was, of course, the Carousel Building. "There will be 14,000 lights on it when it is finished," Korb told Jaeger.

"More like 16,000," Jordan said.

It turns out they both underestimated. The Carousel debuted on Easter weekend in 1981, and was an immediate sensation. A May, 1981 article in the <u>Richland</u>

World's Largest Carousel. Photo from the House On The Rock archives.

<u>Observer</u> called it "the result of two solid years of work, (representing) an investment of $2.8 million."

The estimate of its current value is closer to $4.5 million. It is in all probability the largest Carousel in history, with — today — over 20,000 lights and 269 hand-crafted carousel animals. The Carousel is 35 feet tall, 80 feet wide and weighs 35 tons.

While that sounds impressive, there is no way statistics can do it justice. As the <u>Richland Observer</u> wrote shortly after the Carousel Building opened in 1981, when the lights "are turned on and the massive structure begins to rotate, the visual effect is stunning and quite spectacular."

The paper continued: "The Carousel has imaginative one of a kind creations from the artisans in the House On The Rock's workshop. These animals include dragons, caribous, centaurs, mermaids, tigers, elephants, a huge bulldog, and a unique seahorse-unicorn . . . It is trimmed at the top with 18 handcrafted peacocks. The area directly behind the Carousel is lined with 1,740 square feet of mirror which adds to the flamboyance of the vision."

While the Carousel held a great many animals, Jordan had collected nearly a thousand over the years, and so had several hundred left over. His solution was to mount them on the abundant wall space of the Carousel Building, providing a sensation of a stampede of carousel animals, which was typical of Alex's creativity.

The Richland Observer noted: "Most of these animals are very rare, authentic, antique carousel animals, while some of the animals that line the walls are reproductions of carousel animals crafted in the House's workshop.

"A massive band organ will be brought into the room and mounted adjacent to the Carousel to provide the traditional lilting carousel music . . .

"Three steam engines add to the gay carnival atmosphere. They've been altered with canopy lights and ornamentation similiar to the engines seen in circuses and carnivals of old."

Just six months after the Carousel Building opened, in October of 1981, Alex Jordan opened the exhibit that some call strange and bizarre, and others proclaim as his masterpiece. In any case, the Organ Building is impossible to ignore.

Jordan asked Tom Kupsh to make a doorsized Devil's head that would mark the entrance to what he had originally planned to call the Inferno Room.

At some point Jordan changed his mind. The Organ Building is now based loosely on the work of the 18th Century Italian engraver and draftsman, Giambattista Piranesi.

Milwaukee Journal writer Dave Hendrickson, who in 1989 wrote an article for the paper's Sunday magazine subtitled, "How a Skeptic Came to Like the House On The Rock," said this about the Organ Room: "...(it's) a place where Rube Goldberg meets Jules Verne.

Under the watchful eye of Alex Jordan, Tom Every and crew begin initial construction of the Organ Room. Photo from the House On The Rock archives.

"The Organ Room makes you feel as though you are in the Nautilus, Captain Nemo's submarine in '20,000 Leagues Under the Sea.' And that's odd, because the room doesn't really have a nautical flavor — with the exception of a 2½ story marine diesel engine attached to a man-sized propeller and a huge ship's wheel. That may sound like an overwhelming presence, but it quickly gets lost in the Organ Room.

"The room is crammed with huge copper vats and bronze fittings that seem like they should join together somewhere, pieces of old and unidentifiable electrical equipment, curved iron walkways and spiral staircases, many inaccessible; that lead nowhere. (Tom Every collected many things for this room from who knows where.)

"And, of course, there are the organs for which the room is named. Organ pipes are everywhere . . . There are three organ consoles in the room. One is a genuine antique theatre organ. One was made for the House On The Rock. One is just a joke. You figure it out."

Hendrickson finished his piece by asking if the House On The Rock would ever be finished. His conclusion?

"Nobody who knows Alex Jordan thinks so."

8   **One Last Hurrah**

The next year, 1982, the House opened its refreshment gardens, and a young woman named Julie Esser got a job there selling soda.

Over the next several years, she would become one of Jordan's most trusted employees, rising to public relations director, a post she holds today.

Jordan was fortunate to have put his trust in her, for as his health deteriorated, he would rely on her more and more. He was hospitalized several times during the 1980s. During these times, he was concerned not so much about himself, but about Jennie being home all alone. Esser helped ease his concerns by driving Jennie back and forth from the hospital and helping Jennie while Alex was recovering. "Alex was like a grandfather to me," stated Esser. She really misses the conversations she and Alex would have while he'd eat his lunch in her office. Current events were usually the topic of conversation, with the Jim and Tammy Faye Bakker television ministry scandal always a favorite.

In the early 1980s, Jordan met a young woodworker who would do a number of projects for the House On The Rock. For Mike Olp, the association was more important than that. Olp developed a deep respect for Jordan as a kind man and a creative wonder.

Olp had a shop in Brooklyn, Wisconsin where he made miniature sleighs. He'd sold a couple to Jordan through a third party, and eventually summoned the courage to visit the House and meet Jordan personally.

"I was wondering when you were going to show up," Jordan said.

The sleigh Olp had brought along was too big for Jordan's needs, but he ordered some smaller ones. Then he took Olp over to the House, which the wood-worker had never seen.

"I had never been through it before," Olp recalls. "I was utterly amazed and flabbergasted by all that I saw."

Olp began building miniature sleighs for Jordan on a regular basis and Alex would often stop by Olp's shop.

"He was a wonderful man," Olp says. "He'd come down to my shop on Fridays and look over what I'd done. I think he looked forward to it."

One of the first things Jordan said was, "Mike, you didn't make your shop big enough."

"What do you mean?" Olp replied. "I build miniature sleighs. It's fine."

Recalling the conversation recently, Olp laughed and said, "Well, two years down the road I was building steam carriages and I had to build them in pieces because they were too tall. Alex was right. He must have had an idea I'd be doing other things for him."

One of the steam carriages provided a fun moment for Olp. He had managed to find some old iron and pipe to make it look as realistic as possible. But with the wheels and pulleys on one side, he'd had to build it himself and try to make it look old.

"It looked pretty convincing," Olp recalls.

Jordan looked at it and said, "Mike, where did you get it?"

"I was dumbfounded," Olp recalls. "It was great. I had fooled Alex. Of course he didn't say another word. It was the one time I turned the tables on him."

Jordan took to calling the woodworker "Sir Michael of Olp". For his part, Olp's fondness for Alex was such that he named his two boys after him — Alexander Jonathan and Matthew Jordan.

The years between 1982 and 1987 continued the spirited growth that began in 1981 with the opening of both the Carousel and Organ Buildings.

The focus was largely on collections — in reality, col-lections of collections. In 1984, the Doll House building opened, and the Dodgeville newspaper made the an-nouncement on their front page, calling it "the largest

One of the many doll houses while under construction. Photo by G.B. Telfair.

collection in the world of wooden dollhouses and miniature homes."

The paper continued, "The collection, on exhibit in a building all its own, features 250 architecturally perfect miniatures. They represent many different designs and styles, from antebellum Southern mansions and English townhouses to Victorian palaces, a log cabin, a western saloon, and a Depression era gas station." It was the hard work of Virginia Reynolds and her dedicated crew that was able to put each doll house together and then furnish each house with every detail imaginable.

Two collections, each opened in 1987, have their roots in the historic Tower of London. The Crown Jewel collection features breathtaking replicas of the famous jewels housed in the Tower.

The armour collection features suits of armour made for the House by the curator and staff at the Tower of London. Gothic armour and Samurai armour from the time of the Shogun are on display, along with a diorama of Hannibal crossing the Alps.

Both the armour and Crown Jewel collection were acquired for Alex by Steve and Liz Murray. Liz had become the secretary for the House On The Rock when Gladys Walsh retired. Liz's husband, Steve, ran the concessions at the House On The Rock during this time as well.

In the summer of 1984, work began on a project Alex Jordan had been dreaming about for four decades. In the '40s he had written, in a poem about the house he hoped to someday have, a line that said "one long thin room will hang in space."

He first mentioned it publicly to Wisconsin Trails magazine in 1962, at which time he referred to it as a "space sitting room". The Capital Times newspaper reported that in the mid-'60s, Jordan had a plan for "an all-wood room extending 60 feet into the Wisconsin air."

By 1984, building technology had improved to the extent that when work began on the Infinity Room, Jordan could use metal, steel and glass in a wind and weight forgiving braced-box construction, counterbalanced by 105 yards of concrete.

Architect Rolf Killingstad drew up the plans for this unique undertaking and got the project approved by the state. Dave Nelson Steel Erectors, however, really brought the project to life. Dave Nelson and his daring men virtually hung out over the Wyoming Valley and completed the framework, under the watchful eye of the creator, Alex, of course.

On October 14, 1985, 14 months after construction began, the Infinity Room opened to a somewhat leery, but unquestionably awed, public. Finished, it extends 218 feet out over the Wyoming Valley, and its 3,264 windows and plexi-glass window in the floor give visitors an unequaled view of the surrounding forest (and, on a clear day, the Baraboo bluffs 30 miles away).

"An airplane wing with windows," enthused the Milwaukee Journal in 1989. "Although there is some

Dave Nelson's crew begins construction of the Infinity Room. Photo by G.B. Telfair.

rock under the floor, most of the room, like an airplane wing, relies on its internal structure for support. There are no hidden pillars below, no suspension cables above. As a result, on a windy day — well, you know how you can watch the tip of an airplane wing bob in the wind? Take along a strong stomach."

He had finally gotten his long thin room, hanging in space. It was a terrific accomplishment, all the more so because by the time the Infinity Room opened, Jordan was 71 years old. Though he had made a remarkable recovery from the 1964 heart attack in which he'd essentially lost a third of his heart muscle, by the mid-'80s he was suffering recurring coronary problems — angina, a murmur, and, most troubling, congestive heart failure.

Meanwhile, the House On The Rock, bigger and better than ever, demanded more of his time and energy. On-season it's seven days a week virtually from dawn to dusk, and there's really no off season. Winters are spent building and creating for the next opening day.

Despite having talked to WARF, and despite having offers from everyone from the Marriott Corporation to a group that included actor Steve McQueen, Jordan had never seriously thought of selling the House On The Rock. Now he had to.

"He never wanted to sell," says his friend and attorney, John Mitby. "The only time that changed was in the last three or four years of his life. He physically was not able to do the job he wanted to do on a day by day basis. His health was failing. Now he had something like a hundred employees. It was disappointing to him not to be able to be there day in and day out."

Given Jordan's feelings about the House, any prospective buyer would have to have much more than deep pockets. Jordan scrutinized them carefully.

Mitby recalls, "He had a lot of candidates who had an interest in it, groups from all across the United States. Alex wanted somebody with a business background, because he was concerned the House wouldn't grow if it wasn't economically viable. He didn't want somebody who would buy it and take all the money out of it.

"He knew by then the House On The Rock was bigger than him or anybody else in the world. But he felt an obligation to the public to get somebody who would take care of it. He settled on Art. Art knew business, he knew attractions, and he had a family that could work with him."

"Art" was Arthur Donaldson, who had met Jordan and sold him signs during the 1970s, and who by 1986 had built his sign and billboard company into one of the largest in the Midwest.

Donaldson recalls the negotiating process on the House being interesting, if not a little exasperating. Jordan, of course, was anything but an ordinary businessman. They'd had a running banter back and forth for years about the possibility of Donaldson buying the House, but then one day in 1986, Donaldson recalls, "I got an indication that maybe he was serious."

Still, it wasn't easy. The negotiations took two and a half years.

"It was like no other business deal I ever negotiated," Donaldson says. "Alex set the agenda. He'd just say, 'You make me a proposal.' He'd never say, 'I'll sell it to you for X amount.' I'd go back and try to figure out what he had. All he'd say was, 'You get it all. My plans, everything.' Well, his plans were all in his head or on a napkin with a note on it."

Donaldson met with his accountants and attorneys and tried to establish a fair assessment of the House's worth. Eventually he came up with a proposal he took to Jordan.

"Well, yeah, maybe," Jordan said.

They talked back and forth, reached a general understanding, and drew up a rough draft that Donaldson signed. Jordan gave his tentative approval, but didn't sign.

The next step was a meeting in which both sides brought numbers-crunchers: lawyers and accountants. Jordan was silent through the five hour meeting while the money people negotiated. At the end, all thought they had an agreement.

The next day, Jordan called Donaldson. "Art?"

"Yes," Donaldson said.

"The deal's off."

In retrospect, Donaldson thinks Jordan was spooked by all the three-piece suits sitting at the table. He'd never cared for committees.

A year passed, and nothing much happened. By that time, they were good enough friends that Donaldson occasionally stopped by Alex's home. More than once Donaldson said, "Alex, what do you want?" And Jordan would repeat, "Make me an offer."

Donaldson was about to throw in the towel when a friend of Jordan's got in touch with him. "He's ready now. Try one more time."

Donaldson agreed. John Mitby advised him, "Don't use any lawyers or accountants. He'll get spooked again."

Donaldson showed up at Alex's home with a letter of intent, and a tentative figure. "Can we sign this, Alex?" he said.

"Yes," Jordan said.

"But first we have to go see Mitby," Jordan said.

Donaldson didn't know whether to laugh or cry. The two men went to Mitby's office and once again went over the deal.

Alan Jay Lerner is interviewed by Will Morrissey and A. Dent (_sic_) on the 100th time of the satire of _My Man Godfrey_. _Book_

Finally Alex said, "I want $500,000 a year to work for you."

Donaldson swallowed and said okay. "Anything else?"

"I want my gas paid for," Jordan said.

All was ready. Jordan turned to Mitby. "Is this a good deal?"

The attorney replied, "Alex, that's not the question. Are you ready to sell? Do you want to do this? If you do, this is a good deal."

"I want to sell," Jordan said.

And he did. On December 14, 1988, Art Donaldson purchased the House On The Rock.

"Alex had to like whoever was going to buy it," Donaldson says. "He could have made more money by bidding it, but he always said you can't run a place like this by committee. You have to make your decisions and do it. In fact he had a restriction in the contract that I couldn't have partners."

The truth is, for the first year Donaldson did have a partner of sorts — Alex Jordan. Not only did Jordan still care passionately about the House, he was a valuable asset to the new owner, both from a public relations standpoint as the genius behind it, and also from a creativity standpoint.

In the sale agreement, Mitby had inserted a line that said Jordan must be at the House at least one day a month. When Jordan saw that line he said to Donaldson, "What the hell? Don't you want me around the place?"

"Alex," Donaldson said, "your own attorney put that in there."

"Okay," Jordan said.

"You can be there as much as you want to be."

In reality it was a great situation for Jordan. He could come and go as he pleased and spend time with the projects that truly interested him.

"We became closer over the time we worked together," Donaldson says. "I just wish it could have been longer. In a way, he became almost like a dad in the way he treated me. Maybe he didn't always like what I did, but he was very supportive.

"He didn't interfere," Donaldson continues. "Which I give him a lot of credit for. There had to be a few things that bothered him."

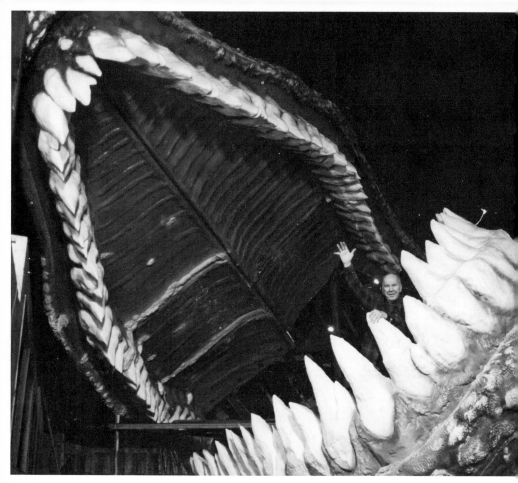

Alex pictured in the Sea Creature's mouth. Photo by Pat Ripp.

After the sale, Jordan spent a lot of time supervising the creation of the Heritage of the Sea Building, which opened after his death in 1990. The highlight of the exhibit is a 200 foot sea creature — longer than the Statue of Liberty is tall — which Jordan loved. Loved? He let himself be photographed in its mouth — for Alex, this was the greatest sacrifice of all.

"The sea creature was the last big project he oversaw," Donaldson says. "He'd sit in an easy chair and bark out his commands. He had the guys going crazy with the creature's eye — which was 60 feet in the air."

One day Donaldson stopped by to see how the sea creature was progressing and found Jordan sitting in his chair.

Donaldson nodded at the creature. "Looks pretty good, Alex."

"No, no," Jordan said. "It's not vicious enough. The eye isn't vicious enough."

Donaldson recalls, "To my knowledge when he passed away it still wasn't vicious enough for him."

Jordan may still have been a perfectionist when it came to exhibits at the House, but by all accounts, in the later years of his life he allowed a gentler side of his personalilty to surface. The bombast was largely gone. Perhaps he was secure in his accomplishments. Certainly there was nothing left to prove.

It's sad he didn't have longer to enjoy his serenity. His body was failing him. In July of 1989, Tom Kupsh, the sculptor who had worked so closely with Jordan in the late '70s and early '80s, came back from Seattle for a visit.

When he saw Alex, he was stunned. "He was a shadow of his former self," Kupsh says. "This was a dying man. He was thin, yellowed, and frail."

On a happier note, Kupsh saw how Jordan had "mellowed out." Alex put his arm around the sculptor and said, "I was hoping you'd come back to work for me."

He took Kupsh on a tour of the new and forthcoming exhibits. "Remember," Jordan said, "when old Alex Jordan told you, 'Don't educate them, entertain them?' "

Kupsh laughed and said yes. And when, a few weeks later, Jordan called him in Seattle and offered him a job, the sculptor said yes.

When he returned to work, Kupsh found an Alex Jordan who was surprisingly gracious. Kupsh recalls: "He began occasionally introducing me to tour guides as the person who had worked with him on many projects at the House On The Rock. 'We worked very hard back then,' he said, 'so you could have all this.' "

Kupsh was touched. "Essentially he was crediting me at the end, which was very nice."

Jordan also talked about future projects. All those years ago they had discussed a room patterned after Dante's Inferno. Now Alex wanted to resurrect it.

"You only live once," Jordan said. "I have all this money. You have all that talent. Let's go for it."

It wasn't to be. "He was deteriorating," Kupsh says. He entered the hospital — Meriter-Methodist in

127

downtown Madison — on October 11, 1989. His doctors had been advising heart bypass surgery for over a year, but he had resisted. Now it was too late. The progressive angina and congestive heart failure were such that a bypass wouldn't help. His doctors even considered a transplant, but found federal guidelines precluded a transplant for someone Jordan's age.

That fall, Art Donaldson was making a buying trip to Thailand. He stopped one day at the House before leaving, and learned Alex was in the hospital. He went to visit, and then he left for Bangkok.

On his return, Donaldson called Jordan at home. Jennie told him Alex was still in the hospital. The next morning, Donaldson called Jordan's doctor. Could he come up to visit? The doctor said yes, adding that they were moving Jordan out of intensive care.

Donaldson thought that was good news; in fact, the opposite was true. Alex had requested it. The end was near.

When Donaldson saw him that morning, his first thought was, "He doesn't look good."

His mind, however, was still sharp.

"Hi, Art," Jordan said. "How are you?"

"Good," Donaldson said.

"How was your trip?"

They talked, off and on, for two hours. Jordan was sedated and would doze off, but he'd awaken and resume the conversation right where they'd left off.

Jennie was coming over in a little while with Julie Esser, Alex said.

As Donaldson was preparing to leave, he said, "You have to get well, Alex, so you can get out there and we can get to those projects."

Alex looked up at him. He gave a small, tired smile. "You've got good people out there," he said. "Don't worry. You don't need me."

Later that day, many of those people had one last chance to say goodbye to the man who, in his last years, had become a father figure in many of their eyes.

Julie Esser and Jennie Olson arrived at the hospital shortly after Donaldson left. They were told the end was near. Jennie had Julie telephone out to the House to tell them if anyone wanted to see Alex, they'd better come today.

About a dozen people came, and it was very moving. Driving into Madison from the House, Neil Hanson, who had worked for Jordan since the 1970s, had a rush of memories.

"In the end he became much more human to me," Hanson says. "For a lot of years he protected us. To make sure we could work year round, he'd start a new building or a new big project so we'd have winter work. By the end it had come full circle. We were protecting him. He fought that, of course. But he'd become a nice older guy who had his extended family out here, and he enjoyed it."

Much of Jordan's "extended family" crowded into his hospital room that afternoon.

"His heart was failing," Hanson says. "You could see it on the monitor. But I was struck by how aware he was. A new person would come in and he'd ask how they were doing. Then he'd drift off."

Later that day, November 6, 1989, Alex Jordan died. He was 75.

Jordan was cremated, and in an emotional private gathering, his ashes were scattered over the House On The Rock. Neil Hanson flew in the airplane from which the ashes were dropped, and recalls how touched the pilot was when she found out why they'd hired the plane.

House employee Doug Finley was in a group of 15 or so standing out on the sun deck that day. They watched the plane and the ashes, and, a little later, House employee Susan Gundlach read a prayer and a poem.

"It was nice," Finley says. "Very nice."

Alex Jordan had indeed come full circle.

9 A Lasting Legacy

On May 1, 1990, the House On The Rock officially opened the Alex Jordan Creative Center, which is both a tribute to Jordan as well as a chance for curious House visitors to have a glimpse behind the scenes of the creative process.

The Home News of Spring Green noted, "The center site is located just a short distance from the House proper, and has long been the place where Alex sat in his chair, directed his staff and planned for more dream worlds to fit into his seemingly never ending fairy castle that has brought millions of tourists to Wisconsin since its opening . . .

"The new center, formerly known as the workshop, is not just one building as one might expect. Instead it is several that house the workers who behind the scenes carry out the late Jordan's creations."

In an interview, general manager Greg Burke told the Home News the center would be "both interesting and educational. It will be a place where people can find out about Jordan, and to understand why he did things the way he did."

He explained that the public would be allowed within touching distance of the creations as they happen, and that people should not expect a neat, orderly environment.

"If there's a jumble of carousel horses being worked on," Burke said, "that's just what the public will see. The horses won't all be standing in line."

Also in 1990, the Heritage of the Sea Building opened. Along with the enormous sea creature, the building also features over 200 museum-sized model ships and a special exhibit of 12-foot-long scale model gunships re-enacting the famous Battle of Trafalgar, which is in the works. (You'll remember that 20 years before, in 1970, one of the books ordered for Jordan by Gladys Walsh was A History of the Combat Vessel.)

In 1991, an animated orchestrion, "The Octupus's Garden," was added to the Heritage of the Sea Building, which will eventually fill it with sound.

Also in 1991, a long-awaited (15 years in the making) music machine, "The Blue Danube," debuted at the House, along with the House On The Rock Carriage Collection, which will still add more nostalgia to the Transportation Building.

Both the Heritage of the Sea and the Blue Danube exhibits were, of course, unfinished at the time of Jordan's death in 1989. The workmen were dedicated to finishing them and finishing them well, as a kind of tribute to Jordan. But it was strange to work without guidance from Alex.

"It was unnerving in a way," Neil Hanson says. "The Blue Danube was visually intact — Alex had done that. We knew he wanted the 'Blue Danube Waltz' to play. But Alex always made the artistic decisions so you always knew exactly how something should look and function. It was hard. I think we got close to what he wanted, but you don't know. I'm sure he would have had an extra touch or two."

Doug Finley helped finish the sea creature. "It was hard not to see Alex sitting there," he recalls. "Everything went pretty smoothly. Tom Kupsh did a fine job. But again, you know Alex would have had some ideas about it."

Another addition was scheduled for late fall and early winter of 1991. Art Donaldson's wife, Karen, has a large collection of Santas — in the thousands — and they will go on display during a special holiday tour. The extended season is something Alex would have appreciated, for many years ago he attemped to have the House open through the 15th of December. The weather, however, didn't cooperate.

In the coming few years, much of the expansion will be inspired by Alex Jordan.

"Alex had several years of planning and construction underway at the time of his death," Donaldson says, "which we've been carrying on. That's going to take a number of years."

While Donaldson has an honest reverence for the genius of Jordan's creative instincts, he thinks the House can be improved in the areas of marketing and promotion, as well as customer service.

"Alex concentrated on creativity," Donaldson says. "We've been concentrating on servicing the customers."

In an interview with the <u>Wisconsin State Journal</u> after he purchased the House, Donaldson said, "No one will ever match Alex's genius and artistry at creating the exhibits we have here and will have here."

But he said he thought he brought some expertise in areas, that while they held little interest for Jordan, were important.

"My role here will be devoted mostly to promotion and improving the amenities of the place to best serve the people," Donaldson said. "We will be doing more joint marketing with other tourist attractions to get our message out in the state and surrounding states."

Even further — Donaldson thinks the House's draw is international. "We are seeing more foreign visitors and want to expand that even further," he said.

Jordan loved to see people come through the door. It was simply the mechanics of marketing he couldn't abide, especially if they interfered in any way with his creation.

One of the few times Jordan ever voiced displeasure to Donaldson after the sale was when Art had struck a very favorable reciprocal trade deal with another popular attraction nearby. The deal called for a sign promoting the other attraction to be placed at the House On The Rock.

It wasn't long before Donaldson got a call.

"Art?" It was Jordan.

"Yes," Donaldson said.

"That sign has got to go. It has got to go." Click.

Donaldson sat down with Jordan and explained that the deal allowed the House On The Rock to have a sign of their own at the other attraction. "A lot of people go through there, Alex," he said.

Donaldson could see Jordan weighing the advantages against the intrusion into his creation.

"Well, it's too bright," he said finally.

"We'll dim it down," Donaldson replied.

"Okay," Jordan said. "One year. Then it has got to go."

In a <u>Milwaukee Journal</u> interview, the president of Tommy Bartlett Inc. offered a prediction the paper said was "shared by many in the tourism industry."

The Bartlett president, Thomas Diehl, said, "You're going to see bigger and better things come out of the House On The Rock with Art Donaldson in charge."

One thinks Alex Jordan would be pleased. He did not choose his successor hastily, and Donaldson, along with his family, most notably his daughter, Susan, have been working hard at the House to earn that trust.

Jordan left the bulk of his estate to Jennie Olson, the woman who shared his life for more than 50 years.

He also left 16 other people — many of them loyal House On The Rock employees — amounts ranging from $50,000 to $250,000.

It may be fair to say that Jordan's biggest beneficiary is the public. He left them the House On The Rock. More than half a million people a year continue to say thank you.

"It's not a business, it's not an ego trip, it's a creative idea," John Mitby says. "And Alex Jordan was the one who breathed life into it."

He brought life to every situation he encountered. Some people didn't like him, but no one could deny the compelling physical presence and tremendous energy that allowed a talented, but unfocused, young man to see the potential in a slab of rock in a remote part of southwestern Wisconsin, to go from picnics with friends on soft summer evenings to a tar paper shack blown away by the wind, and finally, four decades later, to the number one tourist attraction in the state of Wisconsin.

Along the way he made a lot of money, which brought friends, and, inevitably, enemies. People called him cheap, distant, and cruel, and he could be all those things.

But as Tom Kupsh observed, "Who's to be judge of this man?"

Exactly. Perhaps no one can ever fully comprehend another human being, particularly in the case of one

Photo of Don Martin. Photo by G.B. Telfair.

so complex as Alex Jordan. What stands is a life of hard work and accomplishment, of good fortune and bad, friends and feuds — a life above all lived to the hilt.

What stands, too, is his creation, the House On The Rock. Much worse can be said of a man than that, from a standing start of nothing, he brought fun, fascination and excitement to millions.

Don Martin, his employee of 32 years, said, "It's remarkable . . . a little place like this, hidden in the woods, to have become so popular . . ."

In a poignant moment looking back on his career, the boxer Muhammad Ali said, in words all the more eloquent for his poor English, "Ain't nobody done what I did."

Nobody did what Alex Jordan did. His legacy lives.